THE ESSENTIAL
CAKE BOSS™

ALSO BY BUDDY VALASTRO

Cake Boss

Baking with the Cake Boss

Cooking Italian with the Cake Boss

THE ESSENTIAL
CAKE BOSS

(A CONDENSED EDITION OF
Baking with the Cake Boss)

Bake Like the Boss—Recipes & Techniques
You Absolutely Have to Know

BUDDY VALASTRO

ATRIA PAPERBACK

New York   London   Toronto   Sydney   New Delhi

ATRIA PAPERBACK

A Division of Simon & Schuster, Inc.
1230 Avenue of the Americas
New York, NY 10020

First Atria Paperback edition October 2013

ATRIA PAPERBACK and colophon are trademarks of Simon & Schuster, Inc.

For information about special discounts for bulk purchases, please contact Simon & Schuster Special Sales at 1-866-506-1949 or business@simonandschuster.com.

The Simon & Schuster Speakers Bureau can bring authors to your live event. For more information or to book an event, contact the Simon & Schuster Speakers Bureau at 1-866-248-3049 or visit our website at www.simonspeakers.com.

Designed by 3&Co.

Manufactured in the United States of America

10 9 8 7 6 5 4 3 2 1

Library of Congress Cataloging-in-Publication Data has been applied for.

ISBN 978-1-4767-6247-0
ISBN 978-1-4767-4802-3 (pbk)
ISBN 978-1-4767-4803-0 (ebook)

CONTENTS

Introduction

I t all started with a cookie. Everything I am professionally. All that I'm capable of doing in a bakery. Every wedding and theme cake I've ever conceived and created. It all began with the first thing I was ever taught to make when I started working at my family's bakery: butter cookies. It's been a long time since my first "official" day on the job—almost twenty-five years—and it feels like a long time. When I look back over my life and career, I recall my skills growing at the same slow pace at which a tree grows.

A baker's development doesn't happen overnight. It's a painstaking thing. Even if you have raw talent, you have to nurture it, develop it. You have to patiently back up instinct and intuition with craft and, most of all, practice. Because in baking, practice doesn't just make perfect. Practice also lets you move on to the next level, the next challenge, the next thing to be mastered.

Learning to bake is like learning to speak. You pick up that first word, even if you pronounce it imperfectly, and then pretty soon you learn another, and then another. You might not be able to say every word as clearly as a network anchorman, or put words together into sentences, but even as a kid you know that's where you're headed, to a place where you can string words into sentences, sentences into paragraphs, paragraphs into anything you want—an essay, a story, a memoir—if you put in the time to get good at each of the component parts.

It's the same with baking. Those butter cookies were like my first word. They're not difficult to make, and they're still one of the first things we assign to baking newbies at Carlo's Bake Shop, my family's business on Washington Street in Hoboken, New Jersey: You mix a dough of butter, sugar, almond paste, egg whites, and flour; scrape it into a pastry bag; pipe circles of it onto a parchment paper–lined tray; and bake them.

Next to the magnificent theme cakes we produce, those butter cookies might sound like the most idiotproof grunt work you could imagine. But they're not. The beautiful thing about baking is that it all fits together; just as words lead to sentences, and sentences lead to paragraphs, those cookies—as well as the others I made in my first months on the job—laid the foundation for all the baking and decorating that awaited me, and if you're new to baking, they can do the same thing for you.

The **Karate Kid** *Principle*

You've probably already made cookies, but I wonder if you have any idea how much you've learned about pastry and cake making from something as simple as mixing and baking a chocolate chip cookie.

If you've made cookies from scratch, then you already have experience with one of the most important things about baking: mixing dough until it's just the way it's supposed to be. As for the baking itself, you've developed an eye and a nose for doneness, and you've learned a little something about how food behaves after it comes out of the oven, like the effect of carryover heat (the way things continue to cook by their own contained heat as they rest), and that the cookies will harden as they cool.

Those things might not seem like much—I bet you've never even given them much thought—but if you've ever made chocolate chip cookies from scratch, then you've already begun to unleash the baker within.

I call this the "*Karate Kid* principle." In the movie *The Karate Kid*—both the original and the 2010 remake—the young protagonist is forced by his master, Mister Miyagi, to execute a series of seemingly mundane tasks: sanding the floor, painting a house, and waxing a car (in the original) or picking up and putting on a jacket, then taking it off and hanging it up (in the remake). The boy doesn't see the value of these tasks—in fact, he thinks the old man is toying with him—but when it comes time to step up and do some real karate, he finds that he knows all he needs to know: The brushstrokes he used to paint taught him the motion for blocking a blow; bending over to pick up the jacket prepared him to duck; and so on. He's been learning more than he ever realized just by doing those simple little things, over and over.

It's the same with baking: You do small tasks like mixing cookie dough, or piping an éclair full of cream, or rolling out rugelach. It's assembly line work, or at least that's how it seems. But when it comes time to do more intricate baking and decorating, you realize you already know a lot of what's required. If you do enough baking, then you don't even have to think about it because your senses take over: Your fingers know what dough should feel like when you work it; your eyes and nose develop a sixth sense for doneness; and your brain makes adjustments based on the end result so you can correct your course the next time to make it even better.

Once you get all those tasks down to a T, and you move on to the next ones, that's when you have your *Karate Kid* moment. All of those cookie-making skills come into play when you decide to tackle pastry; the mixing, rolling, shaping, and baking have become second nature, so you can save your mental energy for what's new: assembly and decorating. And by the time you get to cake making and decorating, and discover that you've already got the tools to do that . . . well, it's a truly mystical moment in a baker's life when we realize that we possess the skills necessary to make our tools and ingredients do whatever we want them to, and that we're capable of more than we ever thought possible. I hope that this book will help you attain such a moment in your own baking life.

I'm living proof of what I'm talking about. In my early days at Carlo's Bake Shop, I was confined to simple baking tasks such as making cookies and what we call "finishing work," which means slicing and piping pastries full of cream, or topping them with maraschino cherries or strawberry halves. Those jobs didn't seem like much at the time, just your basic dues-paying labor. But eventually, I got so good at these rudimentary tasks that I didn't even have to think about them. By making cookies, I learned how to mix, picked up some simple piping techniques, and honed my eye for doneness, learning to discern the fine lines between "hot," "done," and "burned," which were different for each cookie. By making pastry, I learned a greater variety of skills, developed greater finesse

3

with dough, and began to develop what we call the "Hand of the Bag," the oneness with a pastry bag that you need to be able to decorate cakes. And cakes were the next step in my education.

Because repetition leads to mastery, my favorite times at the bakery were the holidays, when we'd bang out 150 pans of éclairs and 150 of cream puffs in a single day. I used to look forward to those crunch times, because when each one was over, my skills had risen to a new level and I was ready to move on to the next thing. January didn't bring just the new year; on the heels of the December madness at Carlo's, it also brought me new challenges in the kitchen.

I've designed this book to track the same path I took at Carlo's, the one that any young baker still takes there today. Of course, you don't have to bake these recipes in the order I've arranged them in this book, especially if you already have a certain degree of baking and decorating experience. But if you do bake them one after the other, in order—and if you take the time to really learn each recipe until it's second nature to you—when you get to the theme cake recipes, you'll be amazed at how much you know: You will be an expert mixer, and baking will be a breeze. If you are going to use fondant, you'll have already developed crucial rolling skills; and if you're going to do a lot of piping, you'll already know all the techniques required to produce the various effects.

Your Carlo's Bake Shop Apprenticeship

To put all of this another way: Think of this book as your own, private apprenticeship alongside me, the Cake Boss himself. I am going to teach you everything I learned at my family's bakery, in the same order I learned it. We're going to start by making cookies, then work our way up through the Carlo's "curriculum" of pastries, pies, basic cake decorating, and theme cakes.

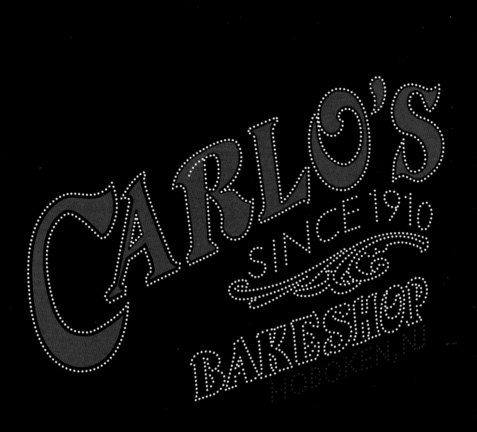

There is going to be a difference between my education and yours, however: I'm not going to make you wait for the larger lessons to reveal themselves. As we take on each recipe in this book, I'll tell you exactly how it will help you with future recipes, so you can flip or think ahead and start to connect the dots for yourself.

Of course, if you already have some baking experience—or even if you don't— you don't have to follow my suggested sequence. You can make all of the recipes in this book without cross-referencing any others in the book, except for the occasional "subrecipe" for a filling, icing, or dough. But if you're starting to bake from scratch, I'd encourage you to confine yourself to cookies for a while, then move on to pastries, then pies, and finally to cakes.

The Pep Talk

Before we get started, I'm going to give you a little talk I like to give to everybody who comes to work with me and my family. Baking is hard work, and in a professional kitchen, it's a team effort. So I think of myself as a coach, and part of my job is to motivate people whenever I can, starting with their first day on the job.

So imagine that it's six o'clock in the morning. You've been up since five. You took a quick shower, pulled on your checkered pants and cook's whites, drove or trained it to Hoboken, and made your way through the predawn streets to the cobblestone alleyway that leads to our back door. You push it open and prepare to step through the looking glass, into your baking future.

The first thing that hits you is the glare. The kitchen is bright. It has to be. We need to be able to discern all the little differences in batters and doughs as they're mixed and in the wide variety of final products as they come out of the ovens.

You spot me waiting for you. Even after all these years, I still love these early morning hours and I'm a bundle of energy and excitement. I take pride in being up and about and hard at work while most of the world is still fast asleep. Most bakers I know feel the same way. These hours are sacred—the streets beyond the bakery walls are quiet; the phones aren't ringing yet. It's the perfect time to commune with our ingredients and our ovens with zero outside distraction. It's the perfect time to bake.

"Hey, how's it going?" I say and we do a high five that turns into a handshake in midair. "Are you ready to work?"

"Yes," you say . . . if you know what's good for you.

"That's what we like to hear," I say. "But before we get you started, let's have a cup of coffee."

We head out to the retail floor and help ourselves to two coffees from the pot behind the counter. On the way back into the kitchen, we pass the picture of my father—Buddy Sr.—hanging over the staircase. The words "Gone But Not Forgotten" are emblazoned across it. And it's true: To this day, his spirit imbues everything we do. His passion and energy inspire everybody who works here—the veterans worked shoulder-to-shoulder with him and the younger generation receives his passion indirectly from the veterans. It's a chain, a continuum, that I hope will never end.

We find a corner of a bench (wooden worktable) where we aren't in anybody's way. As the bakers mix and roll all around us, heaving huge trays of this and that into the ovens, then hauling them out, golden-brown and smelling of sugar and spices, I tell you what I want every new baker to know.

"Within these walls is everything you need to know to be a complete baker." When I say "complete," I emphasize the word so much that you jump a little. "Complete baker" is a term that has special meaning at Carlo's. Everybody who works here takes pride in being a complete baker.

"My cake education was nothing special back when I was a kid," I say. "In those days, everybody in a bakery knew how to do everything. 'All-around bakers,' we called ourselves. Thoroughbreds. There was nothing that we couldn't do. We

baked Tuesday, Wednesday, and Thursday, making everything from biscotti to cakes. Then on Friday, Saturday, and Sunday, when people had their celebrations, we decorated cakes from sunup to dusk.

"Age might be a strike against you in the corporate world," I tell you. "But here, there has always been great respect for the elders, because they've been doing things longer than the rest of us and for the most part are better."

You nod. You look around, and notice that older guys like Danny Dragone—one of our longtime utility players—have no trouble keeping pace with younger guys like my brother-in-law Joey Faugno, who runs the baking department. Both of them are much more than bakers, or even managers; they are founts of baking knowledge and wisdom. They spend a good part of each and every day patiently nurturing young talent by pointing out the things that their charges can learn only through firsthand baking experience, like calling their attention to the distinct textures and colors that let you know when each dough is done mixing. Or how certain cookies need to finish baking out of the oven, on their pan, even though they might seem a little raw. Or that you need to smell the fresh ricotta we still get from a local farm—in pails, on ice, with no labels or expiration dates—before making cannoli cream, to make sure it's not spoiled. We also check up on our young colleagues in more subtle ways—for example, when I see somebody making a wheat pie, I always take a sniff of the filling as it cooks on the stovetop because my nose will tell me whether or not they remembered to include the orange and lemon zest, both of which give off a distinct and potent perfume.

The old pros look so good doing their jobs that new kids can be intimidated and make bad decisions. While I was writing this book, a pair of young bakers burned two racks of cookies. Not burned black, but burned enough that they weren't right to sell. That's a mistake that anybody can make, even me, even today. What matters isn't whether cookies burn, but what you do with them when that happens. In this case, the guys—maybe afraid we'd be cross with them—put the cookies with the properly baked ones that were headed for the pastry cases on the retail floor, which was a big mistake. Fortunately, we caught the burned ones before they went out for sale. They weren't so horribly wrong that they had to end up in the garbage can, but we couldn't sell them, so we donated them to the homeless, which is what we do with the baked goods we produce that aren't quite up to our commercial standards, but are still pretty delicious.

Joey, Danny, and all the other veteran bakers are each like well-oiled machines in their own right. And there's no chit-chat, no clowning around—they are all focused on what they are doing, and on doing it to the best of their ability. One guy might be mixing batch after batch of dough, which we still do in an old industrial Hobart mixer, the baker rolling up his sleeve and sticking his arm down into the depths of the bowl to scrape it; another might be pulling trays off the rotating shelves in the oven, then getting trays of unbaked cookies and pastries onto those shelves before too much heat has escaped; yet another might be doing finishing work, icing cookies or piping éclairs full of cream.

I think about how each of these guys could switch roles or how they could all do the same task if that's what the production day called for. It's an increasingly rare way of doing things.

"Times have changed," I say. "This is the era of specialization. Today, there are guys who just bake, and guys who just decorate. But I think it's best to do it all."

And this is when I look up from my coffee and stare you right in the eye: "That's how we're going to train *you*."

This is also about the time I can tell that a new baker is ready to get going, to get his hands dusty with flour and start making the magic happen. But before I set that person to work, I like to make a few more points, and I want to make them to you before *we* begin baking together.

1. Success in baking is founded on repetition. The most important thing to realize about baking is that repetition is the gateway to greatness. Just as athletes have to train and musicians have to practice, if you want to be a terrific baker, you need to learn to love the process—from measuring out your ingredients to mixing batters and dough to baking to decorating. There's no separating one part from another, because all those steps add up to success in the final product, and if any one of them is suspect, then

the whole thing falls apart. I also think of great bakers as soldiers, because it's all about discipline, about taking great pride in turning yourself into a human machine that can execute the same series of steps over and over in the exactly same way.

2. There are many ways to be creative. On *Cake Boss*, the theme cakes are the center of attention, and with good reason: They are jaw-dropping, showstopping examples of unbridled creativity. Our theme cakes make anybody who sees them, even other professionals, say, "How did they do that?" But there are many ways of being creative. If you don't have the hands for, or interest in, elaborate decorating, but love the flavors and textures of delicious baked goods—and the pleasure those qualities give to the people you bake for—then you might turn out to have a skill for creating your own distinct recipes.

    In other words, don't feel that you have to become a cake boss yourself in order to find happiness in baking; there are countless home bakers out there who take great pride and satisfaction in making nothing but cookies. If that's where your comfort zone and happiness lie, be happy with that and get as good at it as you possibly can.

3. Always be willing to try new things. As much as I believe in repetition and consistency, I also believe that it's important to try new things, to balance the required discipline for baking with a chance to be spontaneous and to grow. Whether it's tinkering with a tried-and-true recipe to see if you can make it even better, or attempting to design something you've never seen before, it's worth the trouble and relatively minor expense to innovate, especially if you end up bringing a new recipe or design into the world.

4. No two bakers are exactly alike. There's no one way to do anything when it comes to baking. The recipes and advice I share work for me, and for my family and coworkers, and for the customers who line up outside our shop on Washington Street in Hoboken, New Jersey. But—who knows?—you might come up with a new way of doing things—from tweaking a recipe to discovering a new use for a kitchen tool—that works for you. At the end of the day, baking is about your own individualistic relationship with the tools

and ingredients; if you can come up with your own way of doing something, don't hesitate to go give it a try. And if you change a recipe, be sure to keep notes on what you did so you can do it again! (See "Keeping a Book," below.)

5. Believe. Along with a good rolling pin and mixer, and a well-stocked pantry, there's something else you need every time you bake: confidence. If you watch seasoned bakers do their thing, they all exude an easy confidence. You need to have the same slight swagger when you step up to your workstation and dust it with flour. You need to know in your bones that you will not fail. Why is this so important? Because you need to trust all your senses; for example, most dough doesn't look anything like what the final product it produces looks like, so you need to have the confidence to know you've mixed it properly. Similarly, when you step up to a naked cake, piping bag in hand, and get ready to go to work on that blank canvas, if you have any doubt in yourself, it will be reflected in imperfect borders and wavy lines. Believe in yourself when you bake and decorate; it's as important as anything else.

Keeping a Book

All professional bakers keep a notebook full of hard-won baking wisdom—everything from recipes for the signature items in the shop where they work to old family treasures they want to be sure survive through the ages. But you can't necessarily pick up a baker's book and use it like a cookbook, because a lot of us, especially the veterans, keep our notes in a form of code, changing at least one ingredient so that nobody can steal from us.

My favorite story about this tradition involves one of the legends of Carlo's Bake Shop, Mike Vernola, better known as Old Man Mike. Mike's encrypted recipes were almost as revered as the man himself. To keep a young, up-and-coming baker from ripping off his secrets, Mike always changed the quantity of one ingredient in a recipe; for instance, an ounce of salt might be represented as twelve ounces of salt. There was no rhyme or reason to it; one recipe would have the flour wrong, another the sugar. And only Mike knew the correct quantities.

One day, a job applicant was trying out with us, and he managed to get his hands on Mike's book. Somebody saw him take it into the bathroom, and—worried that Mike's intellectual property was being lifted—reported it to me. I tracked down my father with great urgency and reported what was going on. Rather than freak out, he let loose with a roar of laughter.

"What's so funny?" I asked.

"He's got Mike's book," my father said. "Nothing's written down right. He won't be able to use any of it!"

Now, that's a funny story, but—in all seriousness—I encourage you to keep your own book. At the very least, you should keep notes in the margins of this and other cookbooks. Maybe you like a little more sugar than I do for a sweeter effect in some recipes; or maybe your oven is a little slower (or faster) than mine, so you want to adjust baking times. Maybe you like to add another spice or chocolate chips to some recipes, or maybe you want to remember to make a dish for a particular person or occasion. Write those things down, all of those things.

If you do a lot of baking, especially if you're a professional or aspiring professional, you should go beyond making notes in a book and start keeping your own notebook. Make it something personal that fits comfortably into your bag or your pocket. Keep notes (they can be shorthand) on recipes, tricks, lessons, and so on. And do yourself a favor: Periodically type those notes up and keep them in a backed-up computer file so that you have them available if you lose the notebook. If you come up with a lot of original stuff, you might even do what the old-timers do and write in code; just be sure you remember what you changed so you can use the recipes yourself!

Equipment

These are the pieces of equipment and tools that you should have on hand if you plan to do a variety of baking with any kind of regularity. For tools exclusively needed for cakes and cupcakes see the list on page 19.

ALL-PURPOSE COOKWARE

BAKING PANS & TRAYS

Baking trays are a great example of my belief that everything matters in a kitchen—they aren't just vessels that hold things during baking; they are a factor in how evenly and controlled the baking process is. I'm not going to name names, but when I visit people's homes, I'm sometimes shocked that people who have otherwise top-notch kitchens treat their baking pans as an afterthought, using paper-thin aluminum trays, sometimes crusted with baked-on food. These don't conduct heat evenly, and cooked-on food will throw smoke in a hot oven. (And that smoke will contaminate whatever you're baking with unwanted flavor.)

I suggest you have at least four pans: two regular 13 by 9-inch pans and two nonstick. If you don't want to buy a nonstick pan, you can purchase a Silpat, a silicone liner that can be laid over the pan. (For a 13 by 9-inch baking tray, you want a Petite Jelly Roll Silpat measuring 11¾ by 8¼ inches.) I recommend that you purchase pans with some kind of rim because you will need it for some recipes, and even when you don't need it, there's no harm in having it there. (The rim also makes a pan easier to grab.) The pans should be made of heavy-gauge metal and be light rather than dark in color (dark material tends to hasten burning), and you should keep them clean by scrubbing with warm, sudsy water; use steel wool on the regular pan and a soft sponge on the nonstick.

COOKIE SHEETS

Similar to my suggested specs for baking trays, cookie sheets should be medium to heavy weight and light in color but also—this is important—rimless, so that heat can evenly bathe the cookies as they bake. (Some sheets have a sloping end that makes it easier to grab them, and to slide cookies off the tray and onto a rack, and that's fine.) Rimless pans don't just allow for better airflow; they also make it easier to check on cookies when they bake, allowing ease of access with a spatula. (At Carlo's, where our oven has rotating shelves, the pans themselves basically circulate, so we use rimmed baking trays for just about everything.) A good, readily available size cookie sheet is 17 by 14 inches, although other sizes are fine so long as they fit in your oven without blocking the flow of air from top to bottom.

MINI MUFFIN TRAY

For making Rum Babas (page 103) and Butterflies (page 97), a nonstick mini muffin tray with 24 wells is essential.

DOUBLE BOILER

A double boiler, which keeps heat from coming into direct contact with the bottom of a pot, is the smart choice to use for melting chocolate and making icing, and for keeping them warm without the risk of scorching them. If you don't have a double boiler, you can set a metal or heatproof glass bowl (such as Pyrex) on top of a pot of simmering water; just be sure the bowl completely seals the top of the pot so steam and heat don't escape, causing the water to evaporate. Sealing is hard to do, and you risk giving yourself a steam burn, so if you plan to make recipes that call for a double boiler, just invest in one rather than using a makeshift one. You'll use your double boiler for nonbaking recipes, too, eventually.

FOR CAKES AND CUPCAKES

CAKE PANS

At home, I generally use a 9 by 2-inch round cake pan. Since many of the cake recipes in this book produce two 9-inch cakes, you'll want to have two pans for baking out of this book. If you plan to make the chiffon cakes on pages 300 to 303, you will need two 7-inch round cake pans.

I like aluminum pans. I know that springform pans are popular, but I don't care for them because they're harder to clean and they're really not necessary. If you grease and flour a pan correctly (see page 133) and let it cool, it will unmold just fine.

CUPCAKE TRAY

For making cupcakes you will need two nonstick cupcake trays with 12 wells each. If you have only cupcake pans that are not nonstick, grease with butter, nonstick spray, or vegetable shortening before baking.

TURNTABLE

A turntable is a positively indispensable piece of equipment for frosting and decorating cakes. For more about this see page 60.

TOOLS

BRUSHES

I recommend that you have 3 types of brushes as part of your kitchen arsenal.

A pastry brush is the best way to apply syrups and other soaking liquids to sponge cakes, to work with melted butter, and to apply water to fondant if you don't have a water pen (see page 118). (A squeeze bottle with a sponge tip applicator or a spray bottle will also work.)

A bench brush has long, stiff bristles and is made for sweeping flour off your work surface. I rarely see these in home kitchens, but I recommend you own one because it makes it very easy to get your surface clean.

A large makeup brush, sometimes called a powder brush, is useful for patting down sugar or cornstarch on your work surface when you are working with fondant. Use it to get any lumps or clumps out of the sugar or cornstarch, whether on your work surface or on the fondant itself.

MICROPLANE ZESTER

In the old days at Carlo's we made our lemon zest by rubbing lemons on one of those old-fashioned box graters. It wasn't the best way to go—the now-familiar recipe instruction not to shave off any bitter pith with your grater wasn't even on our mind—but we didn't know any better. (We also had to garbage the occasional batch when a guy grated a little of his knuckle into the bowl along with the rind!) Then along came the Microplane zester. It's a common kitchen tool today, but was originally devised as a woodworking tool. It's got dozens of minirazors that produce a snowy zest from lemons, oranges, and other citrus fruits.

MIXING BOWLS

Ceramic and glass mixing bowls are perfectly fine options, but I prefer stainless steel for a very practical reason: They don't break if you drop them. Get yourself a good assortment of mixing bowl sizes—generally speaking, I like to use a bowl that's large for a given task because it helps keep ingredients from splashing or flying out of the bowl when you whisk or stir.

PARCHMENT PAPER

Always have some parchment paper on hand: You will use it to line baking and cookie sheets for a variety of items, and I often use a parchment pencil (see page 109) for decorating pastries, pies, and cakes. By the way, if you've ever wondered why some recipes call for parchment paper and some don't, it's almost always a matter of preventing what you're baking from sticking to the bottom of the pan. Parchment can sometimes be left out if you're baking a batter with a high fat content, because it will release just enough fat to keep itself from sticking. (In this book, I don't use parchment in these cases.) Whatever you do, if you don't have parchment paper, don't substitute waxed paper instead. Waxed paper smokes like crazy and will fill your oven and kitchen with that smoke and set off your smoke detector.

PASTRY BAGS

The pastry bag is one of the most important tools for a baker. At Carlo's and in this book, it is are used for everything from piping out cookie dough to filling pastries to icing and decorating cakes.

There are four main types of bag: polyurethane, canvas, disposable, and make-shift. I don't necessarily favor one over the other; instead, I like different bags for different jobs.

For piping cookie dough and thick, heavy batters, the gold standard is a canvas bag, because of its durability. You can really squeeze it, using as much pressure as you like or need to, without fear of busting it open.

For decorating and piping with buttercream, I prefer a polyurethane bag because I find it lets you feel closer to the cream, giving you a greater sense of control.

If you're working with anything that will stain a polyurethane bag, disposable pastry bags are perfectly acceptable to use instead. For example, dark butter-creams such as black, red, and green will all stain a bag, so I recommend a dis-posable bag for working with them.

A makeshift bag isn't really an "official" type of bag, but it can be a lifesaver if you don't have a bag on hand and want to do something that requires it. You can fashion a makeshift bag by using a large (1- or 2-gallon) resealable plastic bag: Fill it with whatever you'll be piping, fold the top closed, and snip off a corner to act as the "tip." You can't get much finesse with a makeshift bag, but it's a perfectly viable way of frosting a cake, filling cannoli, icing cupcakes, and applying meringue to a pie.

A note about working with pastry bags: When you are working with meringue, buttercream, and other sensitive mixtures, the temperature of your hands can cause what's in the bag to soften. Different people's hands have different tem-peratures; mine, for example, tend to generate heat, so after ten minutes of pip-ing, I often squeeze out whatever's left in the bag, then refill the bag with more of whatever I'm piping. If your hands run hot, you may need to do the same.

PASTRY BAG TIPS

At the very least, you should have a #6 plain and a #7 star pastry tip for piping cream, frostings, and fillings. For decorating cakes and cupcakes, a good set of interchangeable decorating tips is essential. There are many sets on the market that feature a variety of tips; you might want to purchase one, or you can amass a collection as you bake more and more recipes, but always check before embarking on a new recipe to be sure you have the necessary tips. You can purchase them individually if necessary, or if you don't want to buy a whole set right off.

Interchangeable tips are small tips shaped to produce specific effects, such as grass, leaves, or the shape that mimics rose petals. You affix these to pastry bags with a coupler that acts as a dock or port for them. In addition to empowering you to create visual effects, tips and bags are also convenient: If you need to create different effects with the same color icing, you don't need to fill different bags; you just change the tip. Throughout the book, I indicate when an interchangeable tip is called for; if a recipe does not indicate "interchangeable," then you just drop the desired tip (a regular pastry tip) into the bag before filling it with the desired filling or frosting.

RACKS

You should have at least two racks for cooling cookies and pastries after baking. (If space on your counter is limited, or you want to avoid resting hot trays on it, you can let the trays cool on top of the racks until the cookies are ready to be transferred.) Racks are available in a variety of sizes; I recommend having at least two nonstick racks, 17 by 12 inches each, which is toward the larger end of the size spectrum.

ROLLING PIN

Everybody in the kitchen at Carlo's has his or her own opinion about rolling pins. There are only two main types of pin (three, if you count polyurethane), but we're as personal about them as a hustler is about his pool stick. Both wooden and marble pins are fine; the overall weight and balance are more important than the material. For rolling out cookie dough, pie crust, and raspberry bars, I like a straight wooden rolling pin. (In reality, I leaned to roll those items with a broomstick, but you don't want to do that at home!) For tougher jobs, such as

rolling out rugelach, pasta frolla to stripe a wheat pie, or puff pastry dough, a wooden, steel, or marble pin with ball bearings that allow the cylinder to spin is better. Those ball bearings help a spinning pin make its way through denser dough. (But I generally use a wooden pin here as well. I've done it so many times that I'm comfortable with it.)

For rolling fondant, I recommend a polyurethane rolling pin because it stays at a good neutral temperature and has a terrific weight for pressing out the fondant, which can become uneven. You don't want to use wood for fondant because wooden rolling pins tend to develop little divots over time, and these will get imprinted into the fondant.

SCALES
Some ingredients are measured by weight rather than volume, so if you don't already own one, I suggest purchasing a kitchen scale. Digital battery-operated scales can be purchased for about $20 and many are small enough to tuck away in a drawer or cupboard when not in use.

SCRAPER
In a home kitchen, a rubber spatula fills in for most of the things we use plastic scrapers for in a professional bakery, namely folding ingredients together and scraping mixtures out of a bowl or a pot. But I still recommend owning a plastic scraper because a spatula keeps you at a bit of a remove from the food you're working with, and sometimes you want to have a greater feeling of control.

In our kitchen at Carlo's, we also use a metal scraper for scraping our benches (wooden work tables), especially for removing caked-on flour. But I don't recommend this tool at home because so many home kitchen surfaces are delicate or prone to scratching.

SIFTER
For ensuring the even distribution of leavening agents such as baking soda and baking powder, and loosening up compacted flour and other ingredients, a sifter is essential. If you don't yet have a sifter and are dying to get started, in its place you can pour your ingredients into a fine-mesh strainer and gently shake it over the bowl into which you are sifting, but the result won't be as fine.

SPATULAS

The three types of spatula called for throughout this book are so different that it seems odd to call them by the same name.

Cookie spatula or pancake spatula: This is probably the first spatula you ever heard of, meant for lifting baked goods out of pans or turning cookies or pancakes as they cook. Sometimes also called a "turner," it's the one we use for checking doneness on cookies and pastries and for lifting them out of their pans.

Icing spatula: Many baking books recommend an offset spatula (aka angled spatula) for icing cakes, but I like a plain old flat icing spatula (we call it a "bow knife" in the Carlo's kitchen), which gives you a greater feeling of control because of its straight shape. I like an 8-inch icing spatula, which I find works well for any task.

Rubber or silicone spatula: This common kitchen tool gets used a lot in baking, mainly for folding two mixtures together or for scraping mixtures out of bowls. It's a good idea to have a set that includes small, medium, and large spatulas in order to be able to accommodate any size job.

STAND MIXER

If you can afford it and have the room for it on your counter, there is simply nothing better for mixing than a good, sturdy stand mixer, which is basically a miniature version of the mammoth industrial mixers we use at Carlo's. You'll need the paddle, whip, and hook attachments.

If you don't have a stand mixer, you can also use a hand mixer for many recipes (I've indicated which ones in the book), but the motors aren't generally as powerful as those on a stand mixer and your arm isn't as durable as the stand itself, so you'll need to take the time to let ingredients such as butter, cream cheese, and shortening really soften before you begin mixing with a hand mixer.

If you do use a hand mixer, set a damp kitchen towel under the mixing bowl to hold it in place. It's a tried-and-true trick that makes mixing much easier than trying to mix with one hand while holding the bowl with the other, especially if you have to pour or drizzle liquids into the bowl while mixing.

In some of these recipes, you can simply use your hands to mix. I'll tell you when that's the best way. Just make sure that your hands are immaculately clean before using them.

THERMOMETERS
For checking the temperature of batters and buttercream, a kitchen thermometer is the only way to go. I suggest that you take advantage of modern technology and purchase an instant-read thermometer that gives you quick, exact, digital information.

It's a good idea to have an oven thermometer to be sure you're baking at the right temperature. Even if your oven reads correctly today, it might begin to run a little hot or a little cold over time. Position your oven thermometer on the same rack you'll be baking on, which will almost always be the center rack.

TIMER
Don't rely on your memory in the kitchen; it's a recipe for disaster. ("Did I put the cake in the oven at 5:45, or was it 5:54?") Get a timer. In particular, I recommend a timer with at least two clocks in case you're doing more than one thing at a time.

WHISK(S)
It's a good idea to have a large and a small whisk on hand for beating mixtures of varying sizes by hand.

WOODEN SPOON(S)
For stirring mixtures as they cook, a wooden spoon or two should be a part of any kitchen arsenal.

Basic Baking Techniques

I'll reinforce all of these points the same way we do at Carlo's Bake Shop—through the actual recipes that follow—but I want to emphasize a few things before we start baking.

MEASURING

The most exact way to measure is by weight, and that's the way we do it in professional kitchens. But since most home cooks are used to measuring by volume (for example, teaspoons, tablespoons, and cups), that's how we tested the recipes in this book. (We still call for weights of some ingredients like fondant, though, to help you be as accurate as possible and to help guide your shopping.) To use the right amount of dry ingredients, when using any kind of measure, use a spatula or straight-edged knife to level off the ingredients. You can use your index finger if necessary, but make sure you don't brush out too much that way.

MIXING

Mixing is probably the least understood, most undervalued part of the baking process, because most people don't appreciate how many variables there are to mixing. It's not just a matter of getting all the ingredients combined; it's also about getting them to come together the right way.

Unless a recipe calls for ingredients to be hot or cold, it's best to go the Goldilocks route and have them just right, by which I mean at room temperature. This is especially true of butter and eggs, whose temperature can have a profound effect on how dough comes together.

Also, always be very careful not to overmix: in many recipes, the dry ingredients are the last to be added; as soon as they are incorporated, stop mixing or you risk ending up with a final product that's tighter, tougher, and more rubbery than you want it to be. The reason? Overmixing activates the protein in the flour and can also produce air bubbles.

Be sure to use the attachment called for in each recipe: the hook, paddle, and whip all produce different effects and are required for specific reasons. Generally speaking, the whip is used when you want to aerate ingredients—such as egg whites—as much as possible; a hook is called on to produce a kneading-like result; and a paddle is the default for just about everything else.

SCRAPING

We have a saying at Carlo's: Bakers scrape. By that we mean that whenever we mix something, we constantly stop the machine to scrape the sides and bottom of the bowl, to be sure that no dry or unmixed ingredients are eluding the hook, whip, or paddle. At home, when using a stand mixer, I recommend that you loosen the bowl so it drops down and you can get your spatula under the mixing attachment. Whenever you see instructions in this book to scrape, I mean to do this; it takes only a few extra seconds, and the result is worth it.

REDISCOVERING THE LOST ART OF ROLLING WITH A PIN

Walk into just about any bakery these days, and you'll see dough being flattened out by a sheeter, a powerful piece of motorized equipment that rolls dough—sometimes massive quantities of it—out into flat sheets. There's nothing wrong with using a sheeter; it's efficient and consistent. But when I was coming up, every baker I knew could achieve with a rolling pin what most young bakers need a sheeter to pull off today.

Home cooks don't have the luxury of using a sheeter, so you really have no choice but to become proficient with a rolling pin if you want to bake at a certain level, and I think that's a wonderful thing, a real link to the craftsmanship that used to define many great home bakers and my trade, and still does at Carlo's and some other tradition-bound bakeries. Rolling dough affects everything from how evenly it bakes to the texture of the final product to how it looks.

One of the keys to working with a pin is: Do not make the mistake of flouring the pin. It looks good, but doesn't really help until deep into the process (see below). Instead, you should flour the work surface beneath the dough and flour the dough itself.

Generally speaking, when rolling with a straight pin—say, rolling out a pie crust—begin rolling up and down the center, then turn the dough sideways and roll over the center again. Then roll just right of center (toward the 1 or 2 o'clock position), then just left of center (toward the 10 or 11 o'clock position). Finally, roll the dough up on the pin, and unspool it over the pie pan.

When working with a ball-bearing pin, roll over the center of the dough heavily to really stretch it out. Then roll the sides down and out to even the dough's thickness. Roll the dough up on the pin, reflour your work surface, then unspool the dough so the side that was touching the work surface is now facing upward. Roll it, starting at the far end and pulling the pin toward you, then back out, first in the middle, then the sides. Continue like this, turning the dough over again and reflouring your work surface (and the pin, if the dough begins to pull or tear), until you achieve the desired thickness.

GETTING THE MOST OUT OF YOUR OVEN

I have lots of admiration for home bakers. Being in a professional bakery, I sometimes take for granted how hard it is to bake from home. At Carlo's Bake Shop, our ovens are works of art. They look primitive: huge, square boxes that are heated from the bottom. But the secret to their success is their rotating shelves that eliminate any hot spots; this is especially important with larger items like cakes, which are more affected by hot spots.

Your home oven might not be as impressive to look at as our monster ovens, but if you get to know it well, and learn its strengths and quirks, you two can make beautiful music together. Here are a few tips.

- Keep it clean.

  When was the last time you cleaned your oven? If you're like most home cooks, the answer is, "Um, well, I'm not really sure . . ." (This is especially unfortunate because I bet 99 percent of you have self-cleaning ovens that make the job a breeze.) Cooked-on food, especially those bits that look like chunks of charcoal fused to the wall or floor of the oven, will throw smoke, and that smoke can show up in the flavor of your baked goods. So be sure your oven is clean, and don't forget to scrub the racks as well; they some-times catch food before it makes it to the oven floor, especially cheese and other sticky foods.

- Seal it up.

  An oven is like your home—if it is not properly insulated, hot air escapes. This probably won't affect your heating bill, but it will throw off your baking time. The cook times in this book assume a nice, steady temperature throughout the process. A well-sealed oven is one way to be sure that's the case. Another is to keep from opening the door during baking; use the oven light and visual cues to monitor doneness as long as possible without allowing heat to escape. When you do open the oven door, get it closed again as quickly as possible.

- Be prepared.

  Preheat the oven before you start baking so it's ready to receive whatever it is you're baking. Before you preheat, be sure the rack is placed where you want it (usually the center).

- Don't overcrowd.

  It's best to bake only one pan of cookies or pastries at a time. At the very least, you should bake on only one rack to ensure even cooking. Try to bake at a time when you can bake each tray on its own for optimum heat circulation.

- Help your oven.

  If you have a small oven, use trays and pans that are smaller than the oven's racks. Do not use pans that totally cover the oven rack, because this will prevent hot air from circulating freely. Because your oven has hot spots, when you're baking sheets of cookies or pastries it's a good idea to turn the pans around midway through the cooking time to ensure even cooking. Also, don't bake partially filled pans of cookies or pastries; the heat won't be distributed evenly and you'll be likely to wind up burning what you're baking. If you have a small batch, gather the pieces in the center of the pan.

Cookies

My baking education started with cookies. They taught me the fundamentals of my craft, and helped me develop muscle memory and intuition to last a lifetime.

But before I get into all that, let me sing the praises of cookies. Carlo's Bake Shop, like most Italian-American bakeries, has a counter section devoted to cookies, and it's the only section that's equally popular with adults and kids. That's because there are precious few new cookies in the world; most of the treats you see under that gleaming glass are exactly the same ones that moms and dads, grandmothers and grandfathers, ate when they were kids, too. The cookies might be something as simple as a black-and-white cookie or rugelach, but I love watching customers dig into them. Their faces say it all—kids are forming taste memories to last a lifetime; grown-ups are reliving their own memories with each bite.

My own memories of cookies date back to long before I ever tried to actually bake anything. When I was a child, my father would often return home from our family business, Carlo's Bake Shop, with a box of tarelles (vanilla cookies) or tea biscuits in hand. Dad was known around Hoboken as a cake master, but it was the cookies that mesmerized me. Most kids feel that way. Cakes are big, towering, intimidating: Before you can eat them, a grown-up has to slice them down to size for you.

But cookies are manageable—you can eat them in just one or two bites. And when I look back at my baking education, it's the same: Cookies were a way of taking in bite-size bits of information about basic skills and techniques, in a way that even a little kid could understand. It was by making cookies that I first learned how to mix dough properly, how to use a rolling pin, and how to start to develop the all-important Hand of the Bag.

The recipes in this chapter produce some of my favorite cookies, and it's a pretty varied bunch that reflects a number of cultures: *pignoli* (pine nut) cookies from Sicily, black-and-white cookies from New York City, Jewish rugelach, and all-American creations such as peanut butter cookies, to name just a few.

For home bakers, a good cookie recipe is a valuable thing. Most cookies can be made quickly and stored for days, if not longer—so you can make them for guests and serve them right out of the oven or keep them on hand for unexpected company. They are also a good project for baking with kids who can do the simple tasks such as adding chocolate chips to dough. In addition to making cookies for family and friends, one of my favorite things to do with cookies is to give them as gifts. Think about giving cookies at the holidays or for a friend's birthday; there's nothing that shows your affection like baking something for someone yourself.

Cookies' simplicity is also the source of their power to teach us about baking. The more simple something is, the more important each part of it becomes. Most cookie recipes are made up of some combination of the same basic ingredients—butter, sugar, flour, eggs, and baking powder and/or baking soda—plus others that add flavor and texture. How those ingredients are mixed has everything to do with how the batter will behave when baked. You don't tend to see mixing discussed much outside professional bakeries, but in a place like Carlo's, we talk about it like it is rocket science. Every cookie requires its own style of mixing: Some need to be mixed quickly, some slowly, some for a long time, some not so much. (My own Achilles' heel as a kid was overwhipping egg whites; I'd let them go until they began to break down, their stiff peaks crumbling like an avalanche in the bowl.) The same is true of pastry and pie dough and cake batter: The difference between an Italian sponge cake batter and a chocolate chiffon batter is profound; being able to understand that begins by learning to understand the differences between the doughs for different cookies.

Cookies are also a good way to begin a baking education because the recipes are more forgiving than those for pastries or cakes. (They also multiply better, so you can double or triple them easily.) What's more, in professional bakeries, cookies are valuable commodities because many of them are convenient: Often, doughs and the finished cookies they produce can be frozen, so we can work them into the production schedule whenever we need to fit them in, and always have cookies on hand or just a few minutes of bake time away. Throughout this chapter, I'll point out when you can take advantage of this same convenience factor at home, so you always have cookies on tap.

Some cookies also teach you how to work with dough, rolling and molding it with your hands, and in some cases with a rolling pin—what we call "bench work" at Carlo's. And they teach the delicate balance between following a recipe and going with your gut in the kitchen. Think back to the first time you baked a chocolate chip cookie. I bet you overbaked it and ended up with something as hard as a manhole cover. That's because you didn't yet know that a chocolate chip cookie has to come out of the oven looking doughy, almost raw. But let it rest for an hour and it firms up to perfection, because the baking soda does its thing as the cookie cools down. We all need to learn the same lesson when it comes to cookies—that we often have to take them out looking a little raw, trusting our baking experience to know that's the right thing to do.

The other, and most overlooked, thing that cookies can teach us is familiarity with our equipment and our ovens. By making cookies, I gained a real intimacy with our oven at Carlo's. This is even more important at home, because your home oven almost certainly has hot spots, and will not cook evenly like a professional oven. Making cookies let me learn that I like working with a broomstick handle for certain doughs (you'd buy a straight rolling pin to get the same effect) and a ball-bearing pin for others; and I learned which type of pastry bag I preferred for different jobs. But there's no one way of doing anything: You might have different preferences, and if they work for you, that's fine with me.

But you won't be able to learn any of that until you get into the kitchen and start baking. So, come on—let's make some cookies!

BAKING IN BATCHES

Even if you have two or more pans, you will need to bake in batches for many of these recipes. Be sure to let the pans cool completely between batches. Putting raw dough on a warm or hot pan can cause the cookies to drop and cause the butter or shortening inside to melt prematurely. It's okay to let the dough just sit while the pans cool—and it's worth it so the cookies come out right.

COOLING COOKIES

It's important to get cookies out of their hot pan and onto a rack as soon as possible after they come out of the oven. Test them with the edge of a spatula to see if they will lift up easily without breaking. As soon as they do, move them. If they are left on the pan too long and become stuck, don't use your spatula like a crowbar; instead, rewarm them briefly in the oven to loosen them up.

STORING COOKIES

Do not put any cookies into a storage container until they have cooled completely. If you put them away warm, their heat will be trapped in the container and the steam will leave behind moisture that will cause them to spoil.

CREAMING

Creaming butter and another ingredient such as almond paste is often the first step in mixing cookie dough and it should not be taken for granted. This base needs to be mixed enough that it aerates, which will set the stage for the cookies to achieve the proper body and texture and help keep them from crumbling too easily. This step often includes a granular ingredient such as sugar that acts almost like sandpaper, smoothing out lumps as early in the recipe as possible.

EGG WHITES

Egg whites are one of the most important ingredients in baking. More than almost any other ingredient, they can determine the density of everything from a cookie to a cake. If you want to understand the effect cooks are looking for in the finished product, note how they tell you to whip your whites: stiff peaks usually means the desired effect is a full-bodied finished product.

In the Chocolate Brownie Clusters recipe (page 51), the whites should be whipped until they are stiff, and that is what allows the batter to expand the way it does. However you whip them, there are a few important things to remember about working with egg whites: First of all, your bowl must be immaculately clean. Wipe it down with distilled white vinegar to get rid of all traces of grease and oil; fat will prevent the whites from stiffening.

BUTTER COOKIES

MAKES 48 COOKIES
{ 24 REGULAR & 24 CHOCOLATE }

These are softer than the butter cookies that come stacked in doilies and sold in round aluminum tins. They're also a little chewier, thanks to the almond paste in the dough. But what they have in common with their popular, mass-produced cousins is that they can be formed into a variety of shapes.

This is one of the first recipes my father taught me to make, so I wanted it to be the first one I share with you. I still remember him showing me how to mix the dough, starting by creaming together the almond paste and butter (this is a crucial step; see "Creaming," page 38), then adding the wet ingredients, and then the flour, mixing and scraping to break up any stubborn lumps. I still hear him coaching me when I make these. "It's all about the *method*," he'd say, explaining that overmixing would cause the cookies to lose their shape and fall like a puddle when baked or be too fragile. He could pull eight hot pans full of these cookies out of the oven so fast the temperature barely dropped, then get the next pans in and on their way. When I tried to match his speed the first time I baked these, removing two trays at once, I scorched my forearm and dropped the pans.

This recipe makes 24 plain cookies and 24 chocolate. You can make them all chocolate by doubling the amount of cocoa, or all plain by leaving it out.

"That's okay, Buddy," he told me. "When you use a knife for the first time you cut yourself; when you do this, you get burned."

2 cups (4 sticks) unsalted butter

1 cup sugar

¾ cup almond paste

4 extra-large egg whites

3½ cups cake flour (no substitutions)

1 tablespoon unsweetened Dutch-process cocoa powder

39

1. Position a rack in the center of the oven and preheat to 350°F.

2. Cream the butter, sugar, and almond paste in the bowl of a mixer fitted with the paddle attachment. (You can use a hand mixer if you allow the butter to soften at room temperature before beginning.) Starting on low speed, and increasing to medium after 2 minutes, paddle the ingredients until uniformly smooth with a mashed potato consistency, about 5 minutes.

3. Lower the mixer speed to low and pour in about one quarter of the egg whites. Paddle for 1 minute, then stop and scrape with a rubber spatula. Paddle on low speed and add another quarter of the egg whites, again paddling for 1 minute, then stop to scrape again. Repeat until all egg whites have been added, paddling for 1 minute extra at the end to ensure the dough is smooth.

4. Add the flour and paddle just until it is absorbed into the dough and the dough is smooth again. (The dough may be wrapped in plastic wrap and refrigerated for up to 1 week, or frozen for up to 1 month; let it come to room temperature before proceeding with the recipe.)

5. Transfer half the dough to a pastry bag fitted with a #7 star tip.

6. Working on one or two nonstick cookie sheets, pipe the dough into 2½-inch circles (see "Practice Makes Perfect: Piping with Steady Pressure," page 49), leaving about 1½ inches between circles, and create four staggered rows of three circles each.

7. Bake the cookies in batches for about 12 minutes or until the bottoms are tinged golden-brown (lift very gently with a spatula to check underneath if necessary) and the star-tip ridges have dropped into a shallow, wavy pattern. Remove the cookie sheets from the oven. As soon as the cookies can be moved, use a spatula to transfer them to a rack and let them cool. (Be sure to let the pans cool completely before piping the chocolate cookies on to them.)

8. Meanwhile, add the cocoa power to the remaining dough and paddle just until blended. Squeeze out any remaining plain dough from the pastry bag, then spoon the cocoa dough into the bag. Repeat steps 6 and 7 with the cocoa dough.

The cookies may be stored in an airtight container at room temperature for up to 2 weeks.

PRACTICE MAKES PERFECT: PIPING WITH STEADY PRESSURE

These cookies call for piping with steady pressure, which will begin training your muscle memory for making cake borders, especially loop borders (see page 105). You can vary the shapes of these cookies, and give yourself practice with other piping techniques; for example, piping straight cookies (about 2 inches long) is a perfect way to work on squeeze-and-pull piping (see page 70).

By the way, here's a tip: Piping consistent circles of any size is harder than it seems. This recipe doesn't call for parchment paper, but until you develop the muscle memory to do this, trace circles on parchment paper in pencil using the mouth of a glass or a cookie cutter as your guide. Turn the paper over so the pencil is on the underside (that is, not touching the dough), line your cookie sheet with it, and use it to trace circles as you pipe. Do this until you find it's no longer necessary, which might be sooner than you think!

DOUBLE CHOCOLATE CHIP COOKIES

{ MAKES 24 COOKIES }

There is nothing subtle about these cookies, which combine a rich, chewy, black-as-night cookie with chocolate chips. You know that popular cake, Death by Chocolate? Well, this is Death by Chocolate that you can fit in the palm of your hand. But don't be fooled by its size; it packs a huge, crowd-pleasing punch of texture and flavor.

The story behind this cookie illustrates the way new recipes come to be in a bake shop. To create it, I began with my dad's chocolate chip cookie recipe. The first order of business was to figure out how to make a chocolate cookie, which you achieve by replacing some of the flour with cocoa. But it's not a simple one-to-one ratio and the only way to solve the problem is by trial and error. I spent hours in the back of the bakery making batch after batch of this, adjusting the quantities of flour to cocoa until I got it just right.

Finally, I came up with this recipe, which I think is one of our very best, and to really put it over the top, I decided to make it with just dark semisweet chocolate chips, rather than a combination of dark and less-rich milk chocolate, which gets lost in the midst of all these strong flavors. It's not often I think I've hit upon perfection—most things can be improved, even if you can't immediately see how to do it—but this, to me, is a perfect cookie. I hope you enjoy it.

1 cup (2 sticks) unsalted butter

1 cup granulated sugar

½ cup light brown sugar

⅓ cup unsweetened Dutch-process cocoa powder

1 extra-large egg

1 teaspoon pure vanilla extract

2 tablespoons whole milk

1¾ cups all-purpose flour

¼ teaspoon baking powder

1 cup semisweet chocolate chips

43

1. Position a rack in the center of the oven and preheat to 325°F.

2. Put the butter, sugar, and brown sugar in the bowl of a stand mixer fitted with the paddle attachment. (You can use a hand mixer if you allow the butter to soften at room temperature before beginning.) Cream on low speed until the mixture is uniformly blended, with no pieces of butter remaining, 2 to 3 minutes.

3. Add the cocoa, egg, and vanilla. Mix on low for 1 to 2 minutes, then stop and scrape with a rubber spatula. Mix on low speed until the mixture resembles chocolate frosting, 2 to 3 minutes. Stop and scrape, then add the milk and paddle for 30 seconds to blend it in.

4. Put the flour and baking powder in a separate mixing bowl and stir together with a fork or whisk. Add to the mixer bowl and paddle on low speed until well mixed, about 1 minute. Scrape and mix for another minute on low speed. With the mixer running on low speed, add the chocolate chips and mix just until evenly distributed, about 1 minute. (The dough can be wrapped in plastic wrap and refrigerated for up to 1 week or frozen for up to 2 months. Let come to room temperature before proceeding with the recipe.)

5. When ready to bake the cookies, break the dough into small pieces and roll between the palms of your hands to form 24 meatball-size balls. Place on two nonstick cookie sheets, about 2 inches apart.

6. Bake until the cookies are flat and hot, 13 to 15 minutes. The cookies will look underdone, but will gently finish baking after you remove them from the oven. Do not leave in the oven for more than 15 minutes, no matter what. Remove the cookie sheets from the oven. As soon as the cookies can be moved, use a spatula to transfer them to a rack and let them cool.

The cookies can be kept in an airtight container at room temperature for up to 3 days. You can continue to eat them for up to 1 week, but they will harden after 3 days. If you want, you can soften them by warming in the microwave for 5 to 10 seconds on the "high" setting.

SIZING UP YOUR COOKIES

When bakers boast of being able to roll or bag portions of dough out uniformly, like a machine, it's much more than a point of pride. All the cookies in a batch should be the same size or they will not cook evenly, and the same is true of pastries. This recipe is a good one for starting to develop that skill because you break the dough up by hand, so if one cookie looks too small or large, you can add to or take away from it. Just be careful not to overwork it as you make adjustments. If you happen to end up with fewer cookies than the indicated yield, that means you have made them too big and the cooking time will probably be slightly longer than indicated; if you end up with too many cookies, you made them too small and the cooking time will probably be shorter.

PEANUT BUTTER COOKIES

{ MAKES 30 TO 36 COOKIES }

This chewy-gooey cookie was devised by my brother in-law, Joey Faugno.

Joey heads up the baking department at Carlo's, and these cookies brilliantly re-create the flavor profile of a peanut butter cup—that irresistible combination of peanut butter and chocolate—by adapting the bakery's recipe for chocolate chip cookies, taking out some of the liquid, and including a combination of peanut butter chips and milk chocolate chips, which get along better than the dark chocolate we use in the original. (Thanks to Joey's fondness for "extra chippy" cookies, these have more chips per square inch than our chocolate chip cookies.)

When baking these, it's crucial to keep carryover cooking (the way foods continue to cook by their own heat after they are removed from the oven) in mind; don't let them spend too much time in the oven. As with a great chocolate chip cookie, you want them to be cooked through but soft and pliable. Use a spatula to peek underneath: As soon as the bottom is lightly browned, get them out.

At Carlo's, we store our peanut butter in the basement, where it can get see-your-own-breath cold in the wintertime, causing the peanut butter to separate and producing a layer of oil on top. So we add an extra step to the recipe, mixing the peanut butter in the mixer to reincorporate the oil before adding the other ingredients. If you refrigerate your peanut butter or have a house as cold as our basement, be sure to do the same.

You can make these with all peanut butter chips, all chocolate chips, or—to really drive home the peanut butter flavor—an addition of chopped, unsalted peanuts.

¾ cup creamy peanut butter

¼ cup vegetable shortening (such as Crisco)

¼ cup tightly packed light brown sugar

1 extra-large egg

One 14-ounce can sweetened condensed milk

1 teaspoon pure vanilla extract

1½ cups all-purpose flour, plus more for flouring your work surface

2 teaspoons baking powder

½ cup milk chocolate chips

½ cup peanut butter chips

½ cup unsalted peanuts, chopped (optional)

1. Position a rack in the center of the oven and preheat to 325°F.

2. Put the peanut butter, shortening, and sugar in the bowl of a stand mixer fitted with the paddle attachment. (You can use a hand mixer if you let the peanut butter soften at room temperature before beginning.) Cream together at low speed to ensure there are no lumps. Add the egg and paddle at medium speed until the ingredients are blended together, about 1 minute. Stop and scrape with a rubber spatula.

3. Add the condensed milk and vanilla extract. Paddle on low speed for 1 minute, stop and scrape, then continue to mix until the mixture is smooth and shiny, about another 30 seconds. Turn off the mixer.

4. Put the flour and baking powder in a small bowl and stir together with a fork or whisk. Add to the mixer bowl. Mix on low speed for about 1 minute. Stop and scrape. Continue to mix on low speed for another minute. Then, with the motor running, sprinkle in the chocolate and peanut butter chips. If you're adding the chopped peanuts, add them at this point. Keep mixing just until the chips are evenly distributed, 30 seconds to 1 minute. (The dough can be wrapped in plastic wrap and refrigerated for up to 1 week or frozen for up to 2 months. Let it come to room temperature before proceeding with the recipe.)

5. Line two cookie sheets with parchment paper, using nonstick spray or a dab of butter in each corner to glue the paper in place. (If you have more than two cookie sheets, line a third sheet to speed up the process of baking in batches.)

6. Flour a work surface and turn the dough out onto the surface. Divide the dough in half. Roll one half out into a cylinder 20 inches long and 1 inch in diameter. Use a knife to cut the dough crosswise into 1-inch segments. (You should have 15 to 18 segments.) Quickly roll each segment into a ball and press down with the palm of your hand until the dough is squeezed down to ½ inch high. (You don't want to take too much time rolling each one or your hands will warm up the dough too much.) Arrange the discs on the pans, about 12 per pan, about 1 inch from the edge and 2 inches apart.

7. Repeat with the remaining dough.

8. Bake the cookies in batches until golden-brown on top and brown at the edges, about 8 minutes. (If they crack a little bit on top, that's all right.) The cookies will still be soft, but the carryover heat will finish cooking them. Remove the cookie sheets from the oven. As soon as the cookies can be moved, after about 10 minutes, use a spatula to transfer them to a rack and let them cool.

These cookies are best enjoyed as soon as they have cooled enough to handle and eat, but will keep for up to 2 days in an airtight container at room temperature.

COOKIE TIPS

MAKING THE CUT

It's tempting to freeze dough in cylinders because we've all seen that slice-your-own ready-made dough in the supermarket. But it's better to freeze raw cookies after cutting them because it will speed the thawing process when you're ready to bake. After cutting them, dust them with flour to keep them from sticking, put them in a freezer bag, and freeze them. When ready to bake, let thaw completely, roll, press, and bake as described in the recipe.

BAKING SODA VERSUS BAKING POWDER

Have you ever wondered why some recipes call for baking soda, some for baking powder, and some for a combination? Baking powder causes batters to rise (the best example is pancakes—they'd be really flat without that smidgen of baking powder in the recipe), while baking soda causes it to drop and spread. It's important to carefully measure all ingredients, but especially something that has such a scientific effect, so be sure to level off the soda in your measuring spoon before adding it to the bowl.

ROLLING BY HAND

Handling the cookie dough here is a good way to start to develop your feeling for working with fondant (see page 117).

CHOCOLATE BROWNIE CLUSTERS

{ MAKES 18 CLUSTERS }

In a bakery like Carlo's, everybody contributes some recipes at some time or another. These cookies—which replicate the flavors and textures of a brownie in a meringue-like cookie that's miraculously crisp on the outside and gooey in the middle—were the invention of the late, great baker Sal Picinich (who passed away while I was writing this book) and they're pretty ingenious.

What impresses me about these cookies is the complex, deeply satisfying result achieved with just a handful of ingredients: egg whites, lemon juice, sugar, cocoa, and nuts. The batter looks like an unholy, goopy-gooey mess. When you make these, you might even think you did something wrong—how could it transform into something appetizing? Your doubt might even be increased by the fact that these can only be spooned onto your baking sheet; the dough is too sticky for a pastry bag and too messy to work with by hand.

But trust me: Once these get into the oven, something magical happens and these ugly ducklings turn into perfect little swans—and everybody will love the way they mimic the flavor and texture of brownies. It's a cookie to die for.

3 extra-large egg whites
½ teaspoon freshly squeezed lemon juice
1½ cups powdered (10X) sugar
¼ cup unsweetened Dutch-process cocoa powder
1½ cups unsalted raw walnut halves

1. Position a rack in the center of the oven and preheat to 325°F.

2. Put the egg whites and lemon juice in the bowl of a stand mixer fitted with the whip attachment. (Be sure the bowl is immaculately clean; see "Egg Whites," page 38.) Whip on low speed for 2 minutes, then on maximum speed until stiff peaks form, about 5 minutes.

3. Sift the sugar and cocoa powder into the bowl together, then fold into the batter with a rubber spatula until the batter is smooth and shiny. Fold in the walnuts, until they are well coated with the batter.

4. Line two cookie sheets with parchment paper, using nonstick spray or a dab of butter in each corner to glue the paper in place. Drop heaping table-spoons of dough ½ inch apart, being sure to include about the same num-ber of walnuts (3 or 4) in each one.

5. Bake until the outside has crisped and the bottom starts to pull away from the parchment paper, 15 to 20 minutes.

6. Remove the cookie sheet from the oven. As soon as the clusters can be moved, use a spatula to transfer them to a rack and let them cool.

Enjoy the cookies right away, or store when completely cool in an airtight con-tainer at room temperature for up to 1 week.

SIFTING

I sift ingredients for two reasons: (1) To be sure dry ingredients aren't too compacted; sifting helps ensure a lighter result in the baked good being made. (2) To better combine two or more dry ingredients that will be added to a recipe at the same time. This is especially important when you are using leavening agents such as baking powder and baking soda—you want those strong-acting ingredients to be as evenly distributed as possible to ensure an even result across the entire baked good. (All of that said, in some cookie recipes I don't call for sifting because the dough gets mixed enough that the ingredients can't help being evenly distributed.)

PIGNOLI COOKIES
{ MAKES ABOUT 48 COOKIES }

Pine nuts, or "pignoli," are a real delicacy that most of us here in America are used to seeing in savory cooking—they're one of the key ingredients in pesto and are often tossed into pastas and other Italian staples to add earthy crunch.

I discovered another use for pine nuts on a trip to Sicily years ago: using them in a cookie that treats them as nuts, the same way we'd use almonds or walnuts here. These cookies would be delicious even without the pine nuts—almond paste, cinnamon, and honey lend an addictively aromatic quality and chewy texture—but the nuts really put these over the top and make them something truly special.

Note that the raw cookies need to rest overnight before baking; otherwise they won't hold their shape and will drop when baked, a lesson that more than a few impatient young bakers have learned the hard way at Carlo's.

By the way, be sure you use almond paste, NOT marzipan for this recipe.

2½ cups tightly packed almond paste (1 pound 9 ounces)
1¼ cups granulated sugar
½ cup powdered (10X) sugar
1 heaping teaspoon ground cinnamon
1 tablespoon honey, preferably clover
1 teaspoon pure vanilla extract
5 extra-large egg whites
5 cups pine nuts (about 1½ pounds)

1. Put the almond paste, granulated sugar, powdered sugar, cinnamon, honey, and vanilla in the bowl of a stand mixer fitted with the paddle attachment. (You can also use a hand mixer.) Paddle at low-medium speed until the mixture is smooth with no lumps remaining, about 1 minute.

2. With the motor running, add the egg whites in three installments and paddle until absorbed, 30 seconds to 1 minute per addition.

3. Cut five 12-inch squares of parchment paper. Arrange a square of parchment paper on a work surface. Put the dough in a pastry bag fitted with a #6 plain tip and pipe the dough out into circles, 2 inches in diameter and about 1½ inches high, leaving about 2 inches between circles . Repeat on four remaining pieces of parchment.

4. Spread the pine nuts out on a cookie sheet in a single layer. Take one of the cookie-dough–covered parchment sheets in two hands and slowly invert it over the nuts. Press down so that nuts adhere to the dough and remove, very gently shaking the parchment to loosen any extra nuts. Set the nut-coated dough aside . Shake the cookie sheet to redistribute the pine nuts, and repeat with the remaining dough-covered sheets until all cookies are coated with pine nuts. Save any unused nuts for another use.

5. Leave the prepared cookies out uncovered at room temperature overnight or for 8 hours to dry.

6. When ready to bake the cookies, position a rack in the center of the oven and preheat to 350°F.

7. Set one of the parchment sheets on a baking tray and bake until the cookies are nicely golden, about 20 minutes. Remove the tray from the oven, carefully transfer the parchment to a heatproof surface to let the cookies cool, and bake the next sheet on the tray. Repeat until all cookies are baked, and let cool for approximately 20 minutes before serving.

The cookies can be held in an airtight container at room temperature for up to 1 week, or wrapped in plastic and frozen for up to 1 month. Let come to room temperature before serving.

Cakes and Cupcakes

Long before I had any idea that they would lead to my own television show, cakes were the Promised Land of my baking existence. When you're a young buck just learning the basics of mixing, baking, decorating, and piping, cakes are what you aspire to, what your entire professional arc is directed toward achieving.

For me, cakes felt like a certain kind of destiny because my father, Buddy Sr., was so renowned for his deft touch with a pastry bag, and for his distinct designs. Dad didn't do the kind of theme cakes we're famous for today—nobody did in those days—but he had a remarkable ability to decorate cakes the way a painter paints on canvas. There was an effortlessness, a weightlessness, to his work—buttercream and whipped cream almost seemed to hover above the cake like clouds; chocolate shavings, too, appeared to dance in the air like confetti; and when he wrote on a cake, well, the words popped like a neon sign. You can teach a baker a lot, but at some point either you're born with great hands or you're not. He had them. So do I.

The good news is that you don't have to be born with the hands of a master to achieve success in cake making and decorating. It's like anything else in baking: If you take the time and effort to get good at the component parts, the big picture is easier than you might have ever imagined.

That said, cake making does require you to pass a number of levels before you're ready to really go for it. Before we get to the theme cakes that any *Cake Boss* fan will want to try, I urge you to have a little patience and develop your basic skills, especially the two most important ones: working on a turntable and developing confidence and accuracy with a pastry bag. In fact, before we go any further, I want to explain a little about both of them and how crucial they are to the decorating process.

THE TURNTABLE

The single most important skill you have to develop for icing cakes and cupcakes is learning to synchronize the trio of yourself, a turntable, and a pastry bag. That probably sounds daunting, but it shouldn't. Because as you're about to find out, the turntable does all the work.

If you want to see the value of a turntable, just try to pipe a neat, even circle on the top of a cake, or even around the side. It's all but impossible to pull off, because you'd have to continually change the angle of the pastry bag, and your wrist simply isn't built for that kind of motion and adjustment. When you use a turntable, however, you create a dynamic similar to a machine: your arm stays in one place, the table turns, and the pressure you place on the bag basically deposits cream or icing on the cake in a uniform manner. Your wrist might turn, or your hand might move up and down to create certain effects, sometimes helped by your leaning forward or back, but your arm will always be stationary. That's why you need a good, sturdy, stainless-steel professional-caliber turntable. Because a turntable does so much of the work, you want one that will endure for years of carrying cakes and spinning round and round.

It doesn't matter which way you rotate a turntable; it can go clockwise or counterclockwise and still produce terrific results. As I said up front, at the end of the day, baking and decorating are largely about your individualistic relationship with your tools and ingredients; whichever direction works for you will get the job done. That said, generally speaking, right-handed decorators tend to turn clockwise; lefties counterclockwise. By the way, before being set on a turntable, cakes should be set on a doily on top of a round piece of cardboard the same diameter as the cake.

USING A PASTRY BAG

When you use a pastry bag, you should fill it about two-thirds full, being sure to squeeze the contents as far down into the bag as possible so they can be forced out of the tip with just the slightest pressure.

The proper way to hold a pastry bag is with one hand, resting the weighty, full part of the bag on your forearm and leaning the back of the bag against your upper arm or shoulder for support. This will keep one hand free for turning a

turntable or performing other side tasks.

Using a pastry bag effectively is all about pressure. Generally speaking, when you use the bag, you will apply either steady pressure, for creating long lines or piping filling and/or frosting, or a pulsating pressure for creating borders and shapes.

There are four main pressure techniques for working with a pastry bag.

- Squeeze-and-pull:
  Just what it sounds like. This technique involves squeezing and pulling the bag upward to deposit the contents in a dab or blob. The classic example is piping cream puff batter; in cake decorating, we use this technique to create bulbs and dots that punctuate cakes and cupcakes.

- Steady pressure:
  This technique, which involves holding the bag for a sustained period of a few seconds, is used to produce a continuous line or circle of frosting or cream, such as the filling for an éclair or the border on a cupcake.

- Steady pressure and movement:
  This technique involves applying continuous pressure to the bag while moving your hand to create a flourish such as a drop line, a swag, or a loop border. (See page 96 for a loop border.)

- Pulse:
  This technique involves all of the above, squeezing and pulling with pulse and movement—for example, to create a shell border (see page 63, bottom photo) around the base of a cake.

ROPE

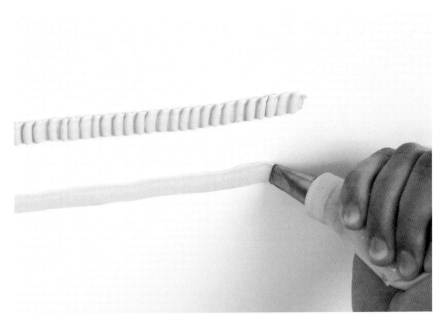

PULSE

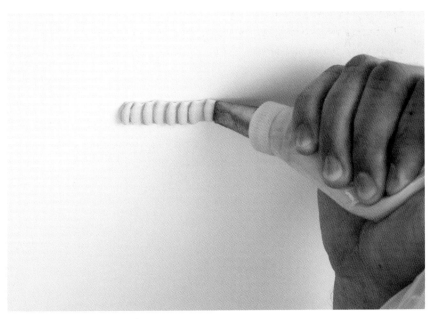

DECORATOR'S BUTTERCREAM

{ MAKES ABOUT 6 CUPS }

Unless otherwise indicated, all of the piping in this section should be executed with decorator's buttercream.

To color the cream, mix food coloring in with a rubber spatula until the cream is uniformly colored. Amounts will vary and will be based on the brand of food coloring and how light or dark your want the cream to be. I recommend food-coloring gel, available in small tubes, because it's less watery and easier to work with. Start with a few drops and add more as you mix. If you are making a dark color, like black, the cream can become loose or watery in which case you should mix in some extra powdered sugar until the texture resembles shaving cream. For white decorator's buttercream, or to dirty-ice a cake (Carlo's-speak for applying a crumb coat) before applying fondant, you do not need to add any color.

7½ cups powdered (10X) sugar
2¼ cups vegetable shortening
6 tablespoons (¾ stick) unsalted butter
1½ tablespoons pure vanilla extract
¼ cup plus 2 tablespoons cold water

1. Put the sugar, shortening, butter, and vanilla in the bowl of a stand mixer fitted with the paddle attachment and paddle at low-medium speed until the mixture is smooth, with no lumps, about 3 minutes.

2. With the motor running, add the water in a thin stream and continue to paddle until absorbed, about 3 minutes.

BUTTERCREAM TIPS

HOW MUCH DECORATOR'S BUTTERCREAM?

In the cake and cupcake decorating instructions that follow, estimated amounts of each color of buttercream required are provided. But no two decorators will use exactly the same amount of buttercream—your roses might be larger or smaller than mine, for example—so don't be worried if you use a bit more or less than is indicated. For most of the cake recipes, the first step is to dirty-ice the cake, which should take approximately 4 cups of buttercream, leaving you 2 cups to color as needed for other purposes such as piping design elements like leaves and grass, and piping a border on the cake. I suggest you dirty-ice the cake before coloring the remaining decorator's buttercream because you can return the icing you scrape off the cake while icing it and making a smooth coating (see page 120) to the bowl with the other uncolored buttercream, which will give you more to work with.

This recipe can be multiplied or divided to produce larger or smaller batches, and leftover buttercream can be refrigerated right in the pastry bag or piped out into another container and refrigerated.

HOW LONG CAN YOU STORE IT?

Buttercream can be refrigerated in an airtight container for up to two weeks.

DECORATING CUPCAKES

Believe it or not, the perfect way to practice synchronizing yourself, a pastry bag, and a turntable is by decorating cupcakes. In fact, if you've never worked with a turntable before, I suggest spending a little time decorating cupcakes because—rather than the all-or-nothing prospect of icing and decorating a cake—a batch of cupcakes gives you twenty-four chances to get better, with minimal damage done if you mess one up.

Carlo's flower-themed cupcakes are one of our signature offerings. Created for Mother's Day years ago, they have become so popular that we now offer them all year long. Not only are they visually pleasing and delicious, but they give you a chance to practice your piping skills, specifically, using a turntable and applying the four different types of pressure. The rose cupcake and Christmas tree cupcakes also provide a chance to practice more three-dimensional piping, which helps train you for similar tasks called for in cake decorating.

All of these cupcakes are generally made with Vanilla Cake (page 134) or Chocolate Cake (page 138), although you could also make them with Red Velvet (page 153) or any other of the basic cakes in this book, with the exception of chiffon cakes or sponge cake.

Note that each cupcake calls for at least three different colors/types of butter-cream or frosting. When possible, you should have each of them made and in its bag with the proper tip attached before beginning. I have provided estimated amounts called for to make twenty-four of each type of cupcake, but you will probably want to make a variety of types each time you decorate a batch of cupcakes, and you can change the colors as you see fit, so don't be bound by my quantities—try different color combinations to create your own signature cupcakes, making more buttercream and coloring it as needed.

CUPCAKE NOTES

- Stay Centered.
  When working on a turntable, be sure to center the cake or cupcake before going to work on it. If it's not centered, you will end up with a "wobble" effect.

- All cupcakes may be kept in an airtight container at room temperature for up to 3 days.

- Most of these call for only 4 cups of decorator's buttercream; you can refrigerate the remaining 2 cups produced by the recipe, or reduce each ingredient by one-third to produce just 4 cups.

- These cupcakes call for both types of pastry tips: The #126 rose tip is a regular pastry tip (that is, the type that you drop into the bag before the buttercream is added); all others are interchangeable tips that require a coupler. Set up all the pastry bags, icings, and tips before you start.

- The colors used for this and the other cupcakes in this section are my suggested colors; feel free to experiment with other colors and combinations to create your own signature look and develop your eye for coordination.

SUNFLOWERS

Sunflowers' unique petals are extra easy to replicate with a piping bag, which makes these look especially lifelike. Your family will do a double-take when you serve these up.

24 cupcakes
1 cup green buttercream, #126 rose tip
2½ cups yellow buttercream, #70 interchangeable leaf tip
½ cup brown buttercream or Chocolate Fudge Frosting (page 161),
    #133 interchangeable grass tip

1. Center a cupcake on the turntable.

2. Take the green buttercream bag in hand and, while turning the turntable, apply steady pressure to pipe a border around the edge of the cupcake.

3. Switch to the yellow buttercream bag, and employ the squeeze-and-pull technique to pull leaves from just inside the border (*not* the center of the cupcake) to just over the edge.

4. Switch to the brown buttercream bag and squeeze and pull little strands in the center of the cupcake.

5. Remove the cupcake from the turntable and repeat with the remaining cupcakes.

PUFF FLOWERS

These might be the easiest and most fun to make of all the flowers. If your kids want to try their hand at piping flowers, these are the ones to do.

24 cupcakes
1 cup green buttercream, #126 rose tip
2½ cups pink buttercream, #10 interchangeable plain tip
½ cup orange buttercream, #8 interchangeable plain tip

1. Center a cupcake on the turntable.

2. Take the green buttercream bag in hand and, while turning the turntable, apply steady pressure to pipe a border around the edge of the cupcake.

3. Switch to the pink buttercream bag, and use the squeeze-and-pull technique to form bulbous shell-like petals, pulling in from the inner edge of the green border.

4. Switch to the orange buttercream bag and squeeze-and-pull a dot in the center of the flower.

5. Remove the cupcake from the turntable and repeat with the remaining cupcakes.

FLAT-PETAL FLOWERS

Unless you have two rose tips, you will need to set up and fill the orange bag after using the green bag. Be sure to clean and dry the tip before dropping it into the bag that will hold the orange buttercream.

1 cup green buttercream, #126 rose tip
2½ cups orange buttercream, #126 rose tip
½ cup yellow buttercream, #8 interchangeable plain tip

1. Center a cupcake on the turntable.

2. Take the green buttercream bag in hand and, while turning the turntable, apply steady pressure to pipe a border around the edge of the cupcake.

3. Switch to the orange buttercream bag and apply the steady-pressure-and-movement technique (rotating your wrist) to create wide petals, starting in the center and ending just inside the border.

4. Switch to the yellow buttercream bag and squeeze-and-pull once in the center of the cupcake to make a dot.

5. Remove the cupcake from the turntable and repeat with the remaining cupcakes.

DAISIES

Daisies scream "summer," which means that these cupcakes are perfect at any time of the year: they can underscore the season in the warm months, and bring a little brightness to gray fall and winter days. For a beautiful effect, you can also use the daisies to decorate a full-size cake of your choice.

24 cupcakes
1 cup green buttercream, #126 rose tip
2½ cups white buttercream, #79 interchangeable lily of the valley tip
½ cup yellow buttercream, #33 interchangeable grass tip

1. Center a cupcake on the turntable.

2. Take the green buttercream bag in hand and, while turning the turntable, apply steady pressure to pipe a border around the edge of the cupcake.

3. Switch to the white buttercream bag and squeeze-and-pull from the center of the cupcake to form petals.

4. Switch to the yellow buttercream bag and finish with a few squeeze-and-pull applications to fill out the center of the flower.

5. Remove the cupcake from the turntable and repeat with the remaining cupcakes.

BUDDY'S CABBAGE ROSES

New decorators at Carlo's tell me these are their favorite to pipe because of the nice slow swirling. Get in the zone!

24 cupcakes
1 cup green buttercream, #126 rose tip
5 cups purple buttercream, #104 interchangeable rose tip

1. Center a cupcake on the turntable.

2. Take the green buttercream bag in hand and, while turning the turntable, apply steady pressure to pipe a border around the edge of the cupcake.

3. Switch to the purple buttercream bag and pipe a conical shape in the center of the cupcake. While rotating the turntable, apply steady pressure, turning your wrist to rotate the pastry tip and create a ruffled effect.

4. Remove the cupcake from the turntable and repeat with the remaining cupcakes.

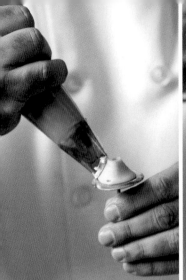
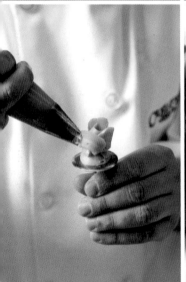

PIPING BUTTERCREAM ROSES

As you can see from the cupcake illustrations, we pipe the flowers directly onto the cupcakes at Carlo's, but you will want to use a rose nail for making roses for both cakes and cupcakes. Piping directly onto cupcakes is best left to the professionals.

1. Take a buttercream bag fitted with the #126 rose tip in your dominant hand and a rose nail in your nondominant hand. Pipe a conical base, 1½ inches high by 1½ inches thick, being sure to release the pressure before lifting the bag from the top of the base.

2. As you rotate the rose nail, hold the bag at a slight angle to the base and apply steady pressure, turning the bag downward to pipe the first rose petal layer, piping all the way around the base.

3. With the bag at a slightly lower angle, pipe three more overlapping petals, but this time pipe only about halfway around the base for each petal.

4. With the bag perpendicular to the rose, pipe five more overlapping petals, wider this time, and piping only about one third of the way around the rose for each petal.

5. Finish by piping five more overlapping layers just under the five piped in step 4.

6. To transfer a rose to a cupcake or cake, put down the pastry bag and pick up a pair of scissors. Open the shears and very gently close them under the rose. Lift the rose off the nail and deposit it in the desired location on the cake, using the edge of the rose nail to gently pull the rose off the scissors.

RED ROSES

Unless you have two rose tips, you will need to set up and fill the red bag after using the green bag. Be sure to clean and dry the tip before dropping it into the bag that will hold the red buttercream.

24 cupcakes
1 cup green buttercream, #126 rose tip
5 cups red buttercream, #126 rose tip

1. Center a cupcake on the turntable.

2. Take the green buttercream bag in hand and, while turning the turntable, apply steady pressure to pipe a border around the edge of the cupcake.

3. Switch to the red buttercream bag, pipe a rose, and transfer it to the top of the cupcake. (For more, see "Piping Buttercream Roses," page 75.)

4. Remove the cupcake from the turntable and repeat with the remaining cupcakes.

CHRISTMAS TREE CUPCAKES

24 cupcakes
1 cup green buttercream, in a bag fitted with the #126 rose tip
5½ cups green buttercream, in a bag set up for an interchangeable tip
½ cup red buttercream, #2 interchangeable plain tip
½ cup yellow buttercream, #3 interchangeable plain tip
¼ cup nonpareils
½ cup white buttercream in a parchment pencil (see page 109)

1. Center a cupcake on the turntable.

2. Take the first green buttercream bag in hand and, while turning the turntable, apply steady pressure to pipe a border around the edge of the cupcake.

3. Attach a #12 plain tip to the coupler of the second bag of green buttercream and pipe a 2-inch-high cylinder. (If you have another color of icing already bagged, you can pipe the cylinder with another color, like white, as pictured. The cylinder will be covered by the leaves, so its color doesn't matter.)

4. Replace the #12 plain tip with the #69 leaf tip and squeeze-and-pull green leaves all over the cylinder.

5. Switch to the red buttercream bag, and squeeze-and-pull small dots all over the tree, representing ornaments.

6. Switch to the yellow buttercream bag, and squeeze-and-pull a "star" (a small "kiss"-like accent) on the top of the tree.

7. Sprinkle nonpareils over the tree. If desired, top each tree with a sugar star, as pictured.

8. Take the parchment pencil in hand and apply steady pressure to pipe 2 strands of white "glitter" in the branches of the tree.

9. Remove the cupcake from the turntable and repeat with the remaining cupcakes.

Note: These cupcakes call for about 8 cups, or 1½ batches, of Decorator's Buttercream.

Working with Cakes

Okay, now it's time to begin working with cakes. In this section, I'll show you how to make the natural progression from trimming and icing cakes to piping techniques to the basics of fondant and then some home versions of the Cake Boss*–style cakes we make on the show.*

The basic cake recipes are found starting on page 133, and basic frostings and fillings on page 159.

TRIMMING AND CUTTING CAKES

Whether you're working with icing or fondant, the first step in decorating any cake is trimming and cutting it. Use a serrated knife to remove the top layer of discolored "skin" of browned cake to make a flat top (see steps 1-3 at right). Because it makes the cake easier to cut evenly, I like to work with a frozen cake. Now, freezing sometimes gets a bad rap in the food world because people associate it with TV dinners and frozen pizzas. But there are times when a freezer can be your best friend. I don't insist on it in the recipes, but freezing a freshly baked and cooled cake is one of the best things you can do. It seals in all the moisture, whereas cakes tend to dry out in the refrigerator. Also, if you plan to ice and/or decorate a cake, it will be firmer when it emerges from the freezer, and you'll have an easier time trimming, halving, and icing it.

Cakes should be frozen for 1 to 2 hours for optimum trimming texture. You can freeze them for longer, but they will become very hard and should be allowed to thaw slightly before you try to cut into them. Do not try to trim a cake that's hard as a rock because the knife can slip, very dangerously. Be sure the cake has a little give to it before you start trimming.

If the cake you're making requires you to cut it in half horizontally, first set it on your turntable or work surface. Kneel or bend so that the cake is at eye level and you can get a good head-on look at it. Keep your eye fixed on the point where the knife enters the cake and as you apply pressure to the top with your free hand, rotate the cake against the knife, keeping it straight to get a nice, even cut. If you will be filling a cake, always try to make the layers level with each other, trimming if necessary so they will rest straight when stacked.

FILLING AND ICING CAKES

I like to use a pastry bag to fill cakes because it's the right tool no matter what filling or frosting you are using—it reduces the amount of spreading and scraping required to neatly fill and ice a cake. If you're using a thick cream for a filling, then using a spatula might cause the cake to break. Similarly, a soaked sponge cake will come apart if you spend too much time working on it with a spatula.

FILLING CAKES

To fill a cake using a pastry bag, fit the bag with the #6 plain tip. Set the first layer of cake on the turntable. Apply steady pressure (see page 62) to pipe the filling in concentric circles, stopping to lift the bag after completing each circle. After the layer is covered with frosting circles, use your cake icing spatula to gently smooth it out into an even layer. Carefully set the next layer on top, gently pressing down to ensure it's nice and level. Then lay down the next layer of filling in the same manner.

ICING (FROSTING) CAKES

Before icing a cake, double-check to be sure the layers look nice and straight and aligned, and be sure the cake is centered on your turntable. Even a four-layer cake should have the same shape as an uncut cake. If necessary, trim the layers to level them, or use a little extra icing under uneven layers to straighten them.

Put the frosting in a pastry bag fitted with a #6 or #7 star tip. You can use either tip for icing a cake; the #7 will give a slightly larger piping effect. For dirty-icing with decorator's buttercream, described on page 120, the #6 tip is the more logical choice.

Spinning the turntable, apply steady pressure to the bag to pipe concentric circles on top of the cake, stopping and lifting the bag between circles. Then, also spinning the table, pipe frosting around the sides, starting at the top and working your way down.

Use the cake icing spatula to smooth the circles on top of the cake together, by holding the spatula parallel to the cake top, and spinning the turntable, gradually lowering the surface of the spatula close to the cake. Turn your spatula perpendicular to the cake and smooth the sides, again gradually moving the spatula closer to the cake. (Note that a decorator's comb was used to produce the ridges on the side of the cake pictured; for instructions on using a decorator's comb, see page 106.)

Finally, while spinning the turntable, hold the spatula parallel to the top of the cake and lower it just to smooth the top one last time to level it off and ready it for decorating.

CAKE NOTES

RATIOS OF FILLING TO CAKE

The appropriate balance of flavors and textures varies from cake to cake, but there are some guidelines that apply most of the time.

Chocolate Ganache (page 166), Italian Buttercream (page 162), Vanilla Frosting (page 160), Chocolate Fudge Frosting (page 161), and Cream Cheese Frosting (page 164) are all rather dense and rich, so the proper ratio of filling to cake is 1:2, meaning a layer of filling should be approximately half the height of a layer of cake.

Italian Custard Cream (page 162), Italian Whipped Cream (page 169), Lobster Tail Cream (page 168), and My Dad's Chocolate Mousse (page 165) are relatively airy and do not threaten to overwhelm the flavor or texture of the cake, so the proper ratio of filling to cake is 1:1, meaning a layer of filling should be approximately the same height as a layer of cake.

SOAKING A SPONGE CAKE

As their name suggests, Italian sponge cakes (see page 142) are made to be soaked with Syrup (page 170). You might snack on a vanilla, chocolate, or carrot cake with no frosting, but you wouldn't do the same with a sponge cake because it's dense and dry until it's been soaked.

To soak a sponge cake, use a pastry brush to generously apply the syrup to the cake, pausing periodically to let the cake soak it up. You might be surprised how much syrup a cake can take on. In layering a sponge cake, do not apply the syrup to the layers until they are on the cake; they will break if you try to lift them after soaking.

A sponge cake will deepen in flavor during a day or two in the refrigerator. Store on a plate, covered loosely with plastic wrap.

FORWARD LOOP

REVERSE LOOP

DOUBLE REVERSE LOOP

LOOP LOOP SKIP

SHELL

ROPE

DOT

"S"

LEAF

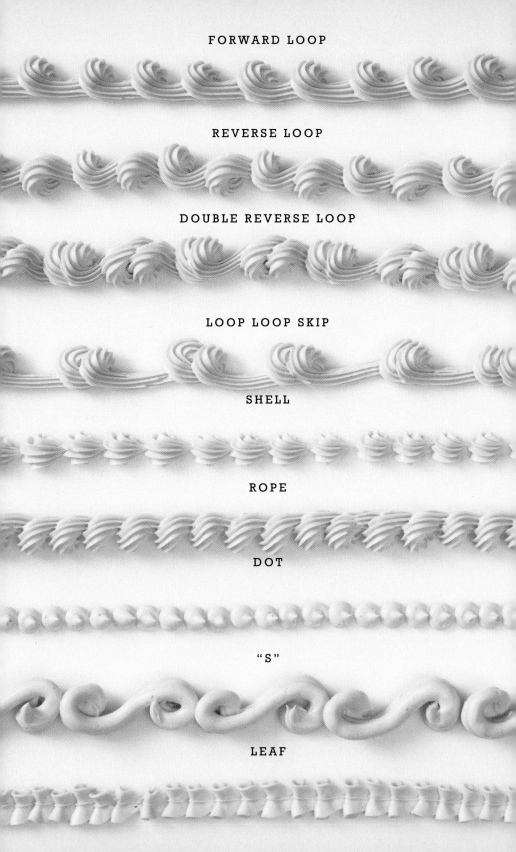

Decorating Techniques

There's no limit to what designs and patterns you can make on a cake, but here are some of the techniques we use most often at Carlo's Bake Shop. If you've never worked with a pastry bag, fondant, or modeling chocolate before, you should be prepared for a period of growth and development, but most people find that they improve quickly. Just be patient, and remember what my father always said: "There's nothing in decorating that you can't fix."

BASIC PIPING TECHNIQUES

On iced cakes, I like to apply a border to both the top and the bottom. Top borders can make a cake look bigger or smaller: If the border is piped inside the edge of the cake, it makes the cake look *smaller*. If the border is piped outside the edge of the cake, it makes the cake look *larger*. My favorite border for the bottom of a cake is a shell border (see page 94). A shell border can be made with a number of different regular or interchangeable tips, and in just about any size or shape.

MAKING BORDERS

A shell border can be made with a number of different regular or interchangeable tips, and in just about any size or shape.

To pipe a shell border (at right and on page 97), position the tip at the bottom of the cake. Squeeze and pull as you slowly rotate the turntable. Continue all the way around until you return to the starting point.

BORDER SHAPES

The basic border shapes are variations on the following shapes: Shell, Loop, Rope, Dot, "S" and Leaf.

SAVING BAGS

Many of my cake designs call for white (uncolored) decorator's buttercream to be used both for dirty-icing the cake and for piping some design elements, usually with an interchangeable tip.

To avoid using two different bags—one fitted with the #6 star tip for dirty-icing, the other with an interchangeable tip—pipe the buttercream for dirty-icing with a bag fitted with the coupler, but no tip, then attach the interchangeable tip called for in the decorating instructions.

OTHER BORDERS

FORWARD LOOP

REVERSE LOOP

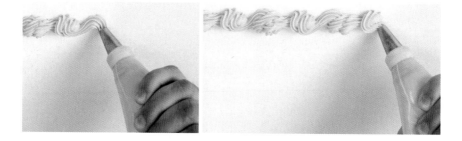

DOUBLE REVERSE LOOP

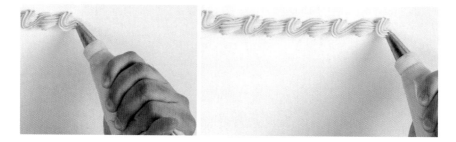

LOOP LOOP SKIP

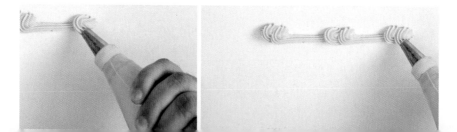

OTHER BORDERS

SHELL

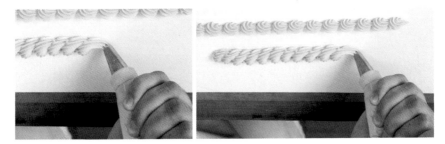

ROPE

DOT

"S"

DECORATION FOR SIDES OF THE CAKE

SWAGS

Use a small interchangeable tip, such as #103. Apply steady pressure and an up-and-down motion with your wrist. Move only the wrist/hand; the arm stays still.

SWAG

PULSE SWAG

SIMPLE SWAG

RUFFLE SWAG

SHELL SWAG

LEAF SWAG

DROP LINES

For drop lines you need perfectly smooth buttercream with no air in it. It should be fluffy and smooth as shaving cream. Use a #2, #3, or #4 plain interchangeable tip.

Keep your arm still and lean away as you turn the table.
Let the line drop, then . . .
lean forward and place the other end of the line on the cake.

Release. Repeat until you return to the starting point.

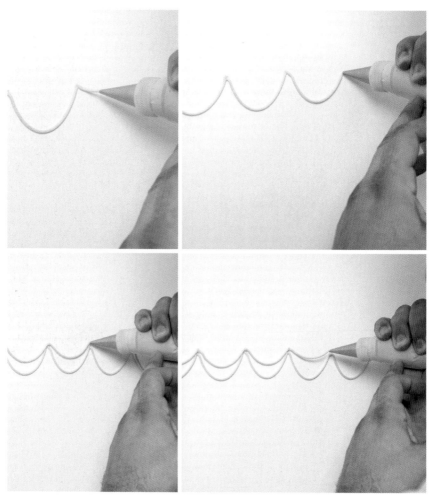

DOUBLE DROP LINES

To make a double drop line repeat the same steps, making slightly shorter drop lines just above the first lines, but ending each drop line at the same point.

You can make variations by adding intersecting drop lines.

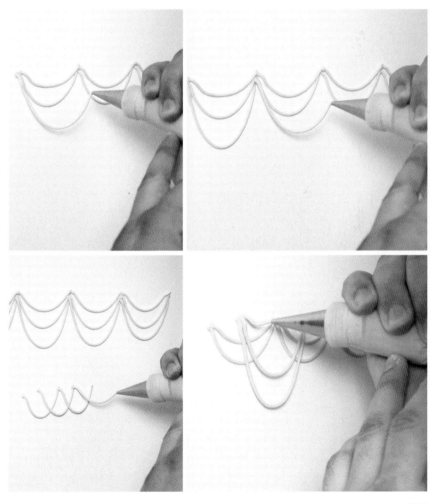

ROSETTES

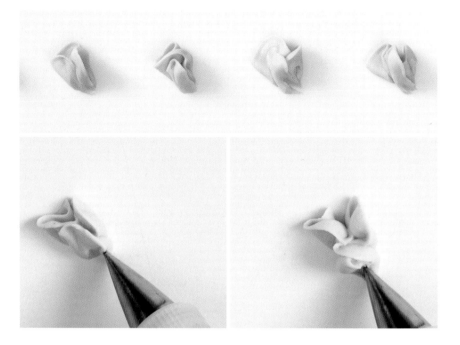

HEARTS

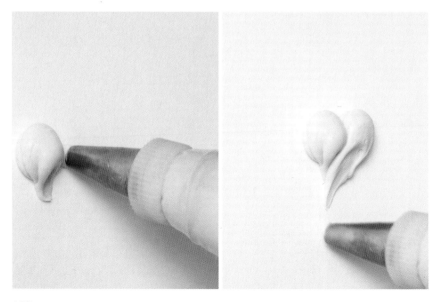

FILIGREE PIPING

I call filigree piping "drawing on the cake." Generally speaking, you want to use a #2 or #3 plain tip. Filigree piping is freestyle piping, but the rule of thumb is to keep the individual design elements from touching each other. Here are some of my favorite filigree patterns.

CHILDREN'S BIRTHDAY CAKES

A BOY'S BIRTHDAY CAKE

Classic birthday cakes are something every baker should be able to make. They offer a chance to put many of the basic cake decorating skills just described to use.

Two 9-inch cakes, and your choice of filling

6 cups white Decorator's Buttercream (page 64) in a pastry bag fitted with the #6 star tip

1½ cups blue buttercream in a pastry bag fitted with the #126 rose tip

½ cup green buttercream in a pastry bag fitted with the #67 interchangeable leaf tip

½ cup blue buttercream in a parchment pencil (page 109)

Decorator's comb (optional)

1. Prepare the cake: Prepare a double-layer cake on a doily-lined cardboard circle, filling it with the filling of your choice, and icing it with white buttercream. If you have a decorator's comb, use it to create a ridged effect along the side of the cake (see "Decorator's Comb," p. 106).

2. Pipe a border around the base: Pipe a large shell border around the bottom of the cake by rotating the turntable and pulsing the white decorator's buttercream bag.

3. Pipe a border around the top: Use the same bag to pipe a single reverse shell border (aka Figure 8 Loop) on top of the cake.

4. Pipe buds: Take the blue buttercream bag in hand and pipe buds between every other loop of the top border, squeezing as you rotate your wrist. Pipe buds along the shell border at the bottom of the cake, aligning them between every other bud at the top of the cake.

5. Make buttercream roses: Make 3 blue buttercream roses (see page 75) and apply them to the back of the cake (see "Face Front," page 110), angling them toward the front by piping a dab of blue buttercream underneath.

6. Add leaves to the flowers: Take the green buttercream bag in hand and squeeze-and-pull leaves onto the cake, beginning under the edge of the flowers and pulling outward. Pipe smaller leaves between the flowers.

7. Write Happy Birthday: Use the parchment pencil to write Happy Birthday, holding the pencil at an angle and writing with continuous pressure. (For more, see "To write with a parchment pencil," page 110.)

8. For an optional finishing touch: Use the parchment pencil to further decorate the cake with little blue dots.

DECORATOR'S COMB

A decorator's comb, also sometimes called a "triangle," can be used to add ridges to the side of a cake. Hold the comb flush against the cake, with the bottom edge against the turntable, and rotate the turntable.

MAKE YOUR OWN PARCHMENT PENCIL

If you don't have a pastry bag on hand, or if all of your bags are filled with colors you aren't using, you can fashion a quick parchment pencil for small jobs such as writing on cakes, drizzling molten chocolate, or fashioning small leaves.

TO MAKE A PARCHMENT PENCIL:

1. Make a parchment triangle: Cut a 12-inch square piece of parchment paper diagonally in half, either with scissors or by laying it on a cutting board or work surface and slicing through it with the tip of a very sharp knife, to create two triangles. You will use only one triangle; save the other for the next time you need a parchment pencil.

2. Make a parchment cone: With one hand, hold the triangle in front of you with the point facing down. Use your other hand to wrap the paper around itself into a cone, coming around twice to use up all the paper.

3. Tighten the cone: Pinch the wide, open end of the cone with your thumb and forefinger and rub your fingers together repeatedly to tighten the cone. It should still be wide at the open end and tightened into a firm, conical shape.

4. Fill the cone: Use a tablespoon or small rubber spatula to fill the cone about two thirds with buttercream icing or melted chocolate. Hold the cone securely so it doesn't unravel and the tip doesn't become wider than you want it.

5. Close the open end: Roll the open end closed over the buttercream, pressing down to pack the cream in tightly all the way to the tip.

6. Cut the tip: Use scissors to snip off the tip of the cone and approximate the effect of a pastry tip. For a plain tip, cut as far up as you need to for the width you desire. For a leaf tip, flatten out the tip by pressing on it and cut a "V" shape.

TO WRITE WITH A PARCHMENT PENCIL:

Hold the pencil at a 45-degree angle, slightly above the cake, and applying continuous pressure, let icing drop onto the cake as you write. If you cannot maintain continuous pressure for the length of time it takes to write a word, stop after a letter, flex your hand, then continue.

TO MAKE LEAVES WITH A PARCHMENT PENCIL:

Cut a "V" at the narrow end of the cone. To pipe leaves, employ the squeeze-and-pull technique, making the leaves wider at the back and tapering toward the front. **Tip:** Put the middle finger of your nondominant hand about 1 inch up from the point of the pencil for support and guidance.

NOTE:

The parchment pencil can be kept at room temperature for up to 2 days.

FACE FRONT

There's always a front and a back to a cake. Unless you are trying to divert attention from an imperfection, it doesn't matter which side is the front, but it's important to establish it so that everything flows in the same direction. For example, when you put flowers down, you want to tilt them toward the front.

A GIRL'S BIRTHDAY CAKE

This proudly feminine cake has been a Carlo's Bake Shop favorite for generations. To make it, we use two kinds of piped borders and swag, plus my own buttercream roses. Every young girl should have this at least once in her life!

Two 9-inch cakes, filled with your choice of filling
6 cups white Decorator's Buttercream (page 64) in a pastry bag fitted with the
    #6 star tip
1½ cups pink buttercream in a pastry bag fitted with the #126 rose tip
½ cup pink buttercream in a parchment pencil (see page 109)
1 cup white buttercream in a pastry bag fitted with the #6 plain
    interchangeable tip
½ cup green buttercream in a pastry bag fitted with the #67 interchangeable
    leaf tip

1. Prepare the cake: Prepare a double-layer cake on a doily-lined cardboard circle, filling it with the filling of your choice, and icing it with white decorator's buttercream, using the bag fitted with the star tip.

2. Pipe a border around the base: Pipe a large shell border around the bottom of the cake by rotating the turntable and applying pulse pressure to the same white buttercream bag.

3. Pipe a border around the top: Still using the same white buttercream bag, pipe a double loop border just inside the edge on top of the cake.

4. Add swags to the side of the cake: Switch to the pink buttercream bag and make swags from the top of the cake about halfway down the side, applying continuous pressure and a wavy motion, turning your hand up and down at the wrist, but keeping your arm still.

5. Pipe a border on top of the cake: Use the parchment pencil to pipe a border just inside the edge of the cake. Angle the pencil toward the cake and squeeze, rotating the turntable and moving your hand to create the design of the frame.

6. Pipe circles where swags meet the top of the cake: Use the white buttercream bag with the #6 plain interchangeable tip to pipe overlapping circles (two or three on top of each other) where the swags meet the top edge of the cake.

7. Make buttercream roses: Use the pink buttercream bag to make three flowers (see page 75) on a rose nail. Make each flower slightly smaller than the previous one. Contour the flowers along the inner edge of the cake and angle each one upward by piping a dab of buttercream under each one before setting it down.

8. Add leaves to the flowers: Take the green buttercream bag in hand and squeeze leaves onto the cake, beginning under the edge of the flowers and pulling outward. Pipe smaller leaves between the flowers.

9. Write "Happy Birthday": Use the parchment pencil to write Happy Birthday to the left of the flowers, letting the pink border frame the words.

Working with Fondant

Fondant is a sugar dough that can be purchased in different colors. Because you usually see it only on professionally decorated cakes, most people assume that it is difficult to work with, but the truth is that for many home bakers and decorators, I daresay it will be easier to manipulate than frosting and buttercream. I strongly recommend Satin Ice brand fondant because its colors are especially vibrant and its texture is always consistent.

There's a lot to recommend fondant: You don't have to mix it yourself, it can be held at room temperature, and you can simply cut shapes from it to make designs—an infinitely easier process than developing that elusive Hand of the Bag.

If you have kids, fondant is also a great way to involve them in decorating because they can cut shapes, even using cookie cutters, which give them a greater chance for success.

KEEP IT CLEAN

Wash your work surface. Fondant is a magnet for anything and everything—crumbs, debris, or anything else on your work surface will become embedded in the fondant. Even if you manage to get these particles out, they will leave little divots in the surface that cannot be patched over cleanly. So before beginning, brush your surface, wipe it down with a damp cloth, then dry it thoroughly.

LOOSEN IT UP

Before working with fondant, knead it for 1 minute to loosen it and activate the gums.

STORING IT

Keep fondant in the airtight container it comes in, at room temperature, until you use it. After removing the portion you plan to work with, store the remaining fondant, if any, in an airtight plastic bag in the tub at room temperature.

FONDANT TOOLS

There's almost no end to the tools you can use to make fondant cakes, and a number of the cakes that follow call for specific cutters and implements. But a good basic set of tools for working with fondant includes the following.

WATER PEN
This professional tool allows you to apply dabs of water that act as glue with fondant. (If you don't have one, in most cases—except when working with very small pieces—you can use a pastry brush to apply water.)

PIZZA CUTTER
And/or sharp, thin-bladed knife, such as an X-Acto or paring knife: For trimming fondant and cutting shapes.

STRIP CUTTER SET
Essential for cutting strips of various sizes from fondant.

SMOOTHER
This iron-shaped device is used to smooth the top of fondant-draped cakes.

RULER
For precision.

PAINT BRUSH
For applying petal dust.

STEAMER
To finish any fondant design, you can steam the fondant in order to evaporate the cornstarch (or powdered sugar) and give it a smooth, shiny look. You can do this with a fabric steamer, or even an inexpensive travel iron. Pass the steamer 1 or 2 inches over the cake, gently waving it to distribute the steam, until the fondant glistens slightly with moisture. Let the fondant air-dry; this should take only a few seconds. Be careful not to let the steamer spit or spray water onto the cake.

There are 3 basic steps to making a fondant cake:

- "Dirty-ice" the cake

- Roll out the fondant

- Apply the fondant

STEP 1: "DIRTY-ICE" THE CAKE

This is the step that all fondant cakes have in common, and it's actually a series of small steps. To "dirty-ice" the cake, means to readying it to receive the fondant. It is Carlo's Bake Shop–speak for what most bakers call a "crumb coat." It refers to a thin layer of Decorator's Buttercream (page 154) that's laid down as a frosting to help fondant "stick" to the cake. (It might be helpful to think of it as a primer coat of paint.) The proper name, "crumb coat," refers to the fact that you can see crumbs through the icing. It's not important that your dirty-icing be perfect, just that it be thin and cover the entire cake.

To dirty-ice a cake, first ice it as you usually would; see "Icing (Frosting) Cakes," page 88. To do this, cut a 4 by 3-inch piece of poster board with very sharp scissors. As you rotate the turntable, hold the edge of the cardboard flush against the edge of the cake. Then turn your attention to the top of the cake, combing in with brushstrokes from the edge of the cake, only halfway across at first, then all the way across. Professional decorators actually prefer this technique because it puts your hands in closer contact with the cake itself, giving you greater control than with a spatula, although less seasoned decorators will probably have greater success icing their cakes in two steps—first using a cake icing spatula, then finishing with the poster board.

Refrigerate the cake until the buttercream stiffens, 30 to 60 minutes.

STEP 2: ROLL OUT THE FONDANT

This is one of the most important steps in working with fondant. As proud as we are of our rolling skills, at Carlo's we use a sheeter to roll out our fondant. At home, you can get a good result working by hand, but it takes some practice and focus.

1. Dust your work surface with cornstarch or powdered (10X) sugar. Some people use flour, which is a fine alternative, but cornstarch is smoother and lighter, and easier to brush or steam off when you're finished.

2. Remove the fondant required from its storage bag/tub. To coat a two-layer, 9-inch cake—which is what most of the cakes in this chapter are—begin with a 3-pound piece. This will be more than you need, but the excess can be returned to the storage bag.

3. Knead the fondant for about 1 minute to activate the gums and make it pliable. If you're working in cold weather, wash your hands in warm water before beginning; warm hands make this job go faster. Just be sure to dry them thoroughly before starting to knead.

4. Dust your work surface with more cornstarch; do this as often as necessary when you work to keep the fondant from pulling or sticking.

5. Flatten out the ball of fondant with the palm of your hand. Begin rolling it, preferably with a polyurethane rolling pin (second choice would be a sturdy, ball-bearing rolling pin), really putting your forearms and weight into the rolling motion. The trick here is to lift the fondant up off the work surface frequently to keep it from sticking; cornstarch helps here, but you need to strike a delicate balance: too much cornstarch will cause the fondant to dry out by drawing out its moisture. The heat from your hands helps with this. Get into the habit of rubbing the fondant constantly to keep it from drying out.

6. Once you have rolled the fondant out to a length of 18 inches, turn the piece horizontally and fluff it, moving it around to pick up excess cornstarch

from the work surface on the bottom. Then roll the other way. As the fondant begins to take on a circular shape, vary the angle of your rolling, first in one direction, then the other. Continue in this fashion until you have rolled a near-perfect circle, 20 to 22 inches in diameter and ⅛ inch thick, or thinner if you're able. The more you turn the fondant, the thinner and more uniform the result will be.

7. Check the fondant for air pockets (bubbles), poking with a needle tool, or a toothpick. After doing this, smooth out the fondant by hand or with a smoother.

STEP 3: APPLY THE FONDANT TO THE CAKE

1. Set the rolling pin at the far edge of the fondant circle and roll it back toward you, spooling the fondant up onto the pin and gently knocking off any excess cornstarch.

2. Bring the pin over the cake, unspooling the fondant and lowering it over the other side, letting it drape over the sides and onto your work surface Smooth the top with a smoother, then pull and press down gently on the sides to make the fondant taut all around.

3. Caress the fondant with your hands to smooth it against the cake, stretching and pulling it tautly over the top and down the sides, turning the cake and using your fingers to be sure it's smooth all over.

4. Use a pizza cutter or sharp, thin-bladed knife such as a paring knife, to cut around the base and remove any excess fondant. Lift the excess ring up and over the cake. Ball up the excess fondant and return it to its storage bag; it can be reused.

5. Put the cake on a turntable. Use a smoother to smooth out the fondant on the top and sides. Inspect the cake; if you find any dry spots (they will appear arid and veined), rub a little vegetable shortening over them, then smooth with the smoother . . . You are now ready to decorate your cake!

MAKING FONDANT CAKES

Ready to make fondant cakes? Before we begin, a few notes:

- The choice of cake and fillings for the following cakes is entirely up to you. Most are best made with vanilla or chocolate cake, but you can try them with other types of cake, such as red velvet or carrot cake.

- The colors of fondant called for in these cakes are all available from Satin Ice, and the names I use track their product names. (In a few cases you will have to knead two premade colors together to create a color called for in a particular cake.) They are available in 1½- and 5-pound boxes. You should decide how much of each color to buy; this depends on what cakes you plan or are likely to make. One argument for buying 5-pound boxes is that properly stored, the fondant will last for 1 year.

  If you buy another brand of fondant, use the pictures that accompany the cakes to determine the closest approximation to the desired color.

  Note that Satin Ice makes two white fondants, vanilla and buttercream. When I call for white fondant in these recipes, I mean the vanilla variety.

There is a list of ingredients, tools, and equipment included for each recipe. But there are certain items you will need for all recipes, so they are not listed. These are:

Cornstarch or powdered (10X) sugar for dusting your work surface whenever you are rolling out fondant (see page 123), or as otherwise indicated
Turntable
Cake icing spatula
Polyurethane or ball-bearing rolling pin
Smoother
Doily-lined cardboard circle

As with the progression of steps that leads from cupcakes to full-size cakes, I suggest making a simple fondant cake first, then moving on to more intricate, complex designs.

GROOVY GIRL CAKE
{ MAKES ONE 9-INCH CAKE }

The Groovy Girl Cake is one we use to teach new decorators the ways of fondant at Carlo's, so they're a good place for you to start as well. As you can see, it is very makeable, even by first timers.

Two 9-inch cakes, filled with your choice of filling
4 cups white Decorator's Buttercream (page 64) in a pastry bag fitted
with the #6 star tip
3 pounds purple fondant
7 ounces pink fondant
7 ounces pastel green fondant
7 ounces yellow fondant
2 ounces dark-chocolate fondant
1 cup yellow buttercream in a pastry bag fitted with the #6
interchangeable tip

TOOLS & EQUIPMENT
Steamer
Daisy cutters, assorted sizes
Water pen or pastry brush

1. Prepare the cake: On a turntable, prepare a double-layer cake on a doily-lined cardboard circle, filling it with the filling of your choice and dirty-icing it (see page 120).

2. Cover the cake: Drape the cake with purple fondant, smooth it in place with the smoother, and trim it (see page 124).

3. Steam the cake: Use the steamer to steam the fondant and make it shiny.

4. Make daisies:

- Roll out the pink, pastel green, yellow, and dark-chocolate fondant ½ inch thick.

- Use the daisy cutters to cut daisies of various sizes out of each color fondant.

- Overlap the daisies, including different color daisies in each stack and using a water pen to glue them to each other, then onto the cake. Make sure to have one or two overlapping daisies flop from the top to the side of the cake.

5. Pipe a border around the base: Using the yellow buttercream, rotate the turntable and pulse the bag to pipe a shell border around the bottom of the cake.

Basic Cakes

The following recipes produce the basic cakes called for in the book. Because it's the most common size called for throughout the book, the recipe yields indicate two 9-inch cakes, but these recipes can also be used to produce two heart-shaped cakes, a 13 by 9-inch rectangular cake, or two Bundt cakes using 8-inch-wide, 3-inch-deep molds.

Note that oven temperatures differ, so be sure to follow the signs for doneness (not just cooking time); depending on elevation, weather conditions, and other factors, baking times can vary. And remember, unless otherwise indicated, it's a good idea to have all ingredients at room temperature; see the note on mixing on page 29.

Many of these recipes feature a yield for cupcakes as well. Bake cupcakes at 360°F to prevent them from crowning.

TO FLOUR A CAKE PAN

To flour a cake pan, first grease with a thin, even layer of unsalted butter, nonstick spray, or vegetable oil, to coat it just lightly. Add a small fistful of flour (about ¼ cup) to the center of the pan, tip the pan on its side, and rotate the pan to coat the inside with flour. Tap the pan gently on your work surface to loosen the excess flour, and return the excess to your flour container. Tap again and discard any lingering flour into the sink or garbage can.

VANILLA CAKE
{ MAKES TWO 9-INCH CAKES OR 24 CUPCAKES }

This is a home version of the basic vanilla cake we use at Carlo's.
The custard is optional, but really makes the cake unfailingly moist.

2½ cups cake flour, plus more for flouring the cake pans

2 cups sugar, plus more for unmolding the cakes

2 cups Italian Custard Cream (page 163), optional

¾ cup vegetable oil

2¼ teaspoons baking powder

1 teaspoon pure vanilla extract

½ teaspoon fine sea salt

4 extra-large eggs

1 cup whole milk

Unsalted butter (about 2 tablespoons), nonstick spray, or vegetable oil
may be used for greasing the cake pans

1. Position a rack in the center of the oven, and preheat to 350°F.

2. Put the flour, sugar, custard cream (if using), vegetable oil, baking powder, vanilla, and salt in the bowl of a stand mixer fitted with the paddle attachment. (If you don't have a stand mixer, you can use a hand mixer, but take extra care not to overmix.) Mix on low speed just until the ingredients are blended together, a few seconds, then raise the speed to low-medium and continue to mix until smooth, approximately 1 additional minute.

3. With the motor running, add one egg at a time, adding the next one after the previous one has been absorbed into the mixture. Stop the motor periodically and scrape the bowl from the bottom with a rubber spatula to integrate the ingredients, and return the mixer to low-medium speed.

4. After all the eggs are added, continue to mix for 1 additional minute to ensure the eggs have been thoroughly mixed in. This will help guarantee that the sugar is dissolved and that the flour has been thoroughly mixed in, which will help produce a luxurious mouthfeel in the final cake.

5. With the motor running on low speed, add the milk, ½ cup at a time, stopping the motor to scrape the sides and bottom between the two additions. Continue to mix for another 1 minute or until the mixture appears smooth. Before baking, be sure the batter is between 70° and 73°F, or the cake will crown. (Test by plunging a kitchen thermometer into the center of the batter; if it is too warm, put the bowl in the refrigerator for a few minutes; if too cool, let it rest at room temperature.)

6. Grease two 9-inch cake pans (2 inches deep) and flour them. (For more, see "To Flour a Cake Pan," page 133.)

7. Divide the batter evenly between the two cake pans, using a rubber spatula to scrape down the bowl and get as much batter as possible out.

8. Bake until the cake begins to pull from the sides of the pan and is springy to the touch, 25 to 30 minutes.

9. Remove the cakes from the oven and let cool for at least 30 minutes, preferably 1 hour. The cakes should be at room temperature before you remove them from the pan.

10. Put a piece of parchment paper on a cookie sheet, sprinkle with sugar, and one at a time, turn the pans over and turn the cakes out onto parchment; the sugar will keep them from sticking.

Refrigerate or freeze (see page 84) until ready to decorate.

VANILLA CAKE COMBINATIONS
{ For Vanilla Cake recipe, see page 134 }

RASPBERRY DREAM CAKE

LAYERS: 3
FILLING: Lobster Tail Cream (page 168), topped with fresh raspberries
RATIO*: 1:2
FROSTING: Italian Whipped Cream (page 169)
OTHER FLOURISHES**: Each cake layer is half of a 9-inch cake; save extra half cake for another use, or crumble by hand and apply crumbs to sides of cake.

NOTES: Between bottom layer and middle layer, and middle layer and top layer, apply a layer of lobster tail cream and arrange raspberries on top in concentric circles starting from the center and working out.

STRAWBERRY SHORTCAKE

LAYERS: 3
FILLING: Italian Whipped Cream (page 169) topped with fresh strawberries
RATIO*: 1:1
FROSTING: Italian Whipped Cream (page 169)
OTHER FLOURISHES**:
I don't like mint on my strawberry short-cake, but if you do, by all means scatter chopped mint over this cake.

NOTES:
Be sure to double the whipped cream recipe because you are using it as both filling and frosting. Thinly slice the strawberries and arrange them over the whipped cream on each layer.

THE OKLAHOMA

LAYERS: 2
FILLING: Chocolate Fudge (page 161)
RATIO*: 1:2
FROSTING: Chocolate Fudge (page 161)

NOTES:
Each layer is a full 9-inch cake. Be sure to double the frosting recipe because you are using it as both filling and frosting.

THE CONTINENTAL

LAYERS: 4
FILLING: My Dad's Chocolate Mousse (page 165) and Chocolate Ganache (page 166)
RATIO*: 1:1
FROSTING: My Dad's Chocolate Mousse (page 165) and Chocolate Ganache (page 166)

OTHER FLOURISHES**:
Each cake layer is half of a 9-inch cake; save extra half cake for another use, or crumble by hand and apply crumbs to sides of cake.

NOTES:
Double the recipes for both mousse and ganache. Put a thick layer (equal to the height of one cake layer) of mousse between cake layers. Ice with mousse and finish by pouring warm ganache over the top.

*Ratio is filling to cake height.
**If no specific flourish is suggested, I encourage you to use your imagination and the techniques you've learned to create your own uniquely styled cakes.

CHOCOLATE CAKE
{ MAKES TWO 9-INCH CAKES OR 24 CUPCAKES }

Another of our most popular basic cakes. As with all chocolate recipes, be sure to use a high-quality cocoa.

1½ cups cake flour, plus more for flouring the cake pans
1½ cups sugar, plus more for unmolding the cakes
½ cup (1 stick) unsalted butter, softened at room temperature
⅓ cup unsweetened Dutch-process cocoa powder
1 teaspoon baking soda
¼ teaspoon baking powder
⅓ cup melted unsweetened chocolate (such as Baker's),
from two 1-ounce squares
½ cup hot water
2 extra-large eggs
½ cup buttermilk
Unsalted butter (about 2 tablespoons), nonstick spray
or vegetable oil, for greasing the cake pans

1. Position a rack in the center of the oven, and preheat to 350°F.

2. Put the flour, sugar, butter, cocoa, baking soda, and baking powder in the bowl of a stand mixer fitted with the paddle attachment. (If you don't have a stand mixer, you can use a hand mixer, but take extra care not to over-mix.) Mix on low speed just until the ingredients are blended together, a few seconds, then raise the speed to low-medium and continue to mix until smooth, approximately 1 additional minute.

3. Stop the motor and pour in the chocolate. Mix for 1 minute on low speed. With the motor running, pour in the hot water. Add the eggs, one egg at a time, adding the next one after the previous one has been absorbed. With the motor still running, pour in the buttermilk. Stop the motor peri-odically and scrape from the bottom with a rubber spatula to be sure all the ingredients are fully integrated, and return the mixer to low-medium speed. Continue to mix for 1 additional minute to ensure the eggs are fully

absorbed. This will also help ensure that all the sugar is dissolved and the flour is thoroughly mixed in, which will help produce a luxurious mouthfeel in the final cake. Before baking, be sure the batter is between 70° and 73°F, or the cake will crown. (If it is too warm, put it in the refrigerator for a few minutes; if too cool, let it rest at room temperature.)

4. Grease two 9-inch cake pans (2 inches deep) and flour them. (For more, see "To Flour a Cake Pan," page 133.)

5. Divide the batter evenly between the two cake pans, using a rubber spatula to scrape down the bowl and get as much batter as possible out.

6. Bake until the cakes begin to pull from the sides of the pan and are springy to the touch, 25 to 30 minutes.

7. Remove from the oven and let cool for at least 30 minutes, preferably 1 hour. The cakes should be at room temperature before you remove them from the pan. Put a piece of parchment paper on a cookie sheet, sprinkle with sugar, and turn the cakes out onto parchment; the sugar will keep them from sticking.

Refrigerate or freeze (see page 84) until ready to decorate.

CHOCOLATE CAKE COMBINATIONS
{ For Chocolate Cake recipe, see page 138 }

CHOCOLATE MOUSSE CAKE

LAYERS: 3
FILLING: My Dad's Chocolate Mousse (page 165), Chocolate Ganache (page 166), and fresh raspberries
RATIO*: 1:1
FROSTING: My Dad's Chocolate Mousse (page 165)
OTHER FLOURISHES**:
Cut extra half cake into eight triangles, shaped like pizza slices. Pipe small rosettes of mousse in 8 spots along perimeter of top, and arrange triangles on an angle, leaning them on the mousse.

NOTES:
Double the mousse recipe. For the filling, first apply the mousse, then a layer of fresh raspberries, then a thin layer of poured ganache.

CHOCOLATE FUDGE CAKE

LAYERS: 2
FILLING: Chocolate Fudge (page 161)
RATIO*: 1:2
FROSTING: Vanilla (page 160)

NOTES:
Double the frosting recipe.

VANILLA DEVIL'S FOOD CAKE

LAYERS: 2
FILLING: Vanilla (page 160)
RATIO*: 1:2
FROSTING: Chocolate Fudge (page 161)

NOTES:
Double the frosting recipe.

BUDDY DELIGHT

LAYERS: 2
FILLING: Italian Whipped Cream (page 169), fresh strawberries and bananas, Chocolate Ganache (page 166)
RATIO*: 1:1
FROSTING: Italian Whipped Cream (page 169)
OTHER FLOURISHES**:
If desired, finish with chocolate shavings.

NOTES:
Double the whipped cream recipe. To assemble the cake, top the bottom layer with whipped cream, then with thin slices of banana and strawberry, and pour a thin layer of ganache on top. Top with the remaining cake, then ice with whipped cream.

LISA'S DREAM CAKE

LAYERS: 3
FILLING: Lobster Tail Cream (page 168) and fresh strawberries
RATIO*: 1:1
FROSTING: Italian Whipped Cream (page 169)
OTHER FLOURISHES**:
Each cake layer is half of a 9-inch cake; save extra half cake for another use, or crumble by hand and apply crumbs to sides of cake.

NOTES:
For each layer of filling, apply a layer of lobster tail cream, then top by arranging strawberry slices in concentric circles starting from the center and working out.

*Ratio is filling to cake height.
**If no specific flourish is suggested, I encourage you to use your imagination and the techniques you've learned to create your own uniquely styled cakes.

141

PAN DI SPAGNA

ITALIAN SPONGE CAKE

{ MAKES ONE 9-INCH CAKE }

As discussed on page 91, you would never eat this cake without soaking it; it's just too dry on its own. But when you spoon or brush a liqueur or syrup over it, it drinks in the liquid in and is transformed.

This recipe produces only one cake because, conventionally, you cut this cake in half, usually filling it with a cream infused with the same liqueur you used to soak it. For the most part, you will make this cake with layers of filling that are equal in height to the layers of cake, but if you use a rich filling like Chocolate Ganache (page 166) or Chocolate Fudge Frosting (page 161), use half as much, to keep the filling from overwhelming the cake.

1½ cups sugar, plus more for sprinkling the parchment paper
5 extra-large eggs
1 teaspoon pure vanilla extract
Drop of lemon oil (optional)
1½ cups cake flour, sifted, plus more for flouring the cake pan
⅓ cup vegetable oil
Unsalted butter (about 1 tablespoon), nonstick spray, or vegetable oil,
    for greasing cake pan

1. Position a rack in the center of the oven, and preheat to 350°F.

2. Put the sugar, eggs, vanilla, and lemon oil (if using) in the bowl of a stand mixer fitted with the whip attachment. (If you don't have a stand mixer, you can use a hand mixer.) Beat starting on low speed and raise to medium. Whip until the mixture is thick, shiny, and ivory in color, and has multiplied several times in volume, approximately 15 minutes. Remove the bowl from the mixer and use a rubber spatula to scrape as much mixture as possible off the whip attachment and into the bowl.

3. Add the flour and patiently fold it in with a rubber spatula. Pour in the oil, and fold in until fully absorbed into the mixture.

4. Grease and flour a 9-inch cake pan pan. (For more, see "To Flour a Cake Pan," page 133.) Pour the batter into the pan, scraping down the sides of the bowl with a rubber spatula.

5. Bake until the cake begins to pull from the sides of the pan and is springy to the touch, 30 to 40 minutes.

6. Remove from the oven and let cool for at least 30 minutes, preferably 1 hour. The cake should be at room temperature before you remove it from the pan.

7. Put a piece of parchment paper on a cookie sheet, sprinkle with sugar, and turn the cake out onto the parchment; the sugar will keep it from sticking.

Refrigerate or freeze (see page 84) until ready to decorate.

ITALIAN SPONGE CAKE COMBINATIONS

{ For Italian Sponge Cake recipe, see page 142 }

OLD-FASHIONED
ITALIAN RUM CAKE

LAYERS: 2 (from 1 cake)
FILLING: Rum Syrup (page 170), Italian Custard Cream (page 163), and fresh strawberries
RATIO*: 1:1
FROSTING: Italian Whipped Cream (p. 169)

NOTES:
Halve cake horizontally. Soak bottom half with syrup and top with custard cream, then sliced fresh strawberries. Top with the other cake half, soak top half with syrup, and ice with whipped cream.

NEW AGE
CASSATA CAKE

LAYERS: 2 (from 1 cake)
FILLING: Strega Syrup, Cannoli Cream
RATIO*: 1:1
FROSTING: Italian Whipped Cream (page 169)
OTHER FLOURISHES**:
Each cake layer is half of a 9-inch cake; save extra half cake for another use, or crumble by hand and apply crumbs to sides of cake.

NOTES:
Garnish on the sides with toasted slivered almonds, if desired.

TRADITIONAL
ITALIAN WEDDING CAKE

LAYERS: 3 (from 1½ cakes)
FILLING: Rum Syrup (page 170), Italian Custard Cream (page 163), Chocolate Custard Cream (page 163)
RATIO*: 1:1
FROSTING: Italian Whipped Cream (page 169)
OTHER FLOURISHES**:
Garnish on the sides with toasted slivered almonds, if desired.

NOTES:
Halve cakes horizontally. Soak bottom layer with syrup, and top with custard cream. Set another layer on top, soak with syrup, and top with chocolate custard cream. Top with final layer, soak with syrup, then ice cake with whipped cream.

*Ratio is filling to cake height.
**If no specific flourish is suggested, I encourage you to use your imagination and the techniques you've learned to create your own uniquely styled cakes.

WHITE CHIFFON CAKE

{ MAKES TWO 7-INCH CAKES }

When it comes to chiffon, I am a pure classicist.

We only do two things with vanilla chiffon at Carlo's Bake Shop: lemon chiffon and strawberry chiffon (one of my mother's favorites), and those are the only two options you'll find in the chart on page 149.

For this cake, you will need two 7-inch round cake pans (3 inches deep). Note that they should be aluminum, and must not be nonstick, or the cakes will collapse while cooling.

2½ cups cake flour
2¼ teaspoons baking powder
¼ teaspoon fine sea salt
1½ cups plus ⅓ cup sugar
6 extra-large eggs, separated
¼ cup vegetable oil
1 teaspoon pure vanilla extract
¾ cup warm water
Distilled white vinegar, for wiping the bowl
1 teaspoon freshly squeezed lemon juice

1. Position a rack in the center of the oven, and preheat to 350°F.

2. Sift together the flour, baking powder, salt, and 1½ cups sugar into the bowl of a stand mixer fitted with the whip attachment. (You can use a hand mixer if you prefer.) Start the mixer slowly to avoid spraying the flour.

3. In a separate bowl, combine the egg yolks, oil, vanilla, and water by hand with a whisk and continue whisking until well mixed.

4. With the motor running on low, pour the egg yolk mixture into the mixer bowl. After 30 seconds, stop and scrape with a rubber spatula. Mix at medium speed until blended together with no lumps, 1 to 1½ minutes.

5. Transfer the mixture to a clean bowl, using a rubber spatula to scrape down the mixer bowl and get as much batter out as possible.

6. Wash and dry the mixer bowl and whip attachment, then wipe them down with distilled white vinegar to remove all traces of grease and oil. Pour the egg whites and lemon juice into the mixer bowl and start whipping on low speed for about 2 minutes. Slowly add the remaining ⅓ cup sugar and whip on high speed until stiff peaks are formed.

7. With a rubber spatula, fold one third of the meringue into the first mixture. Fold in the remaining meringue in two additions.

8. Gently fill two deep ungreased 7-inch cake pans halfway up.

9. Bake until the sides of the cakes pull away from the pans, 30 to 40 minutes.

10. Remove from the oven and allow to cool. Release the cakes from the pans by flipping them upside down and tapping fiercely against a work surface.

The cakes can be refrigerated in an airtight container for up to 3 days or frozen for up to 2 months.

OTHER CAKE COMBINATIONS

{ For Vanilla Cake recipe, see page 134 }

STRAWBERRY CHIFFON

LAYERS: 2 (from 1 cake)
FILLING: Italian Whipped Cream (page 169) and fresh strawberries
RATIO*: 1:1
FROSTING: None

NOTES:
Fill the cake with the whipped cream and sliced fresh strawberries, and ice it with the same. Then garnish with fresh strawberries on top.

CHOCOLATE CHIFFON

LAYERS: 2 (from 1 cake)
FILLING: My Dad's Chocolate Mousse (page 165), fresh strawberries, Chocolate Ganache (page 166)
RATIO*: 1:1
FROSTING: My Dad's Chocolate Mousse (page 165)
OTHER FLOURISHES**:
Dust finished cakes with powdered sugar.

NOTES:
Fill with mousse and berries, then a thin layer of ganache. Ice with mousse. Pipe six rosettes of mousse on top, and set a giant strawberry between each of the rosettes, then drizzle the cake with ganache.

*Ratio is filling to cake height.
**If no specific flourish is suggested, I encourage you to use your imagination and the techniques you've learned to create your own uniquely styled cakes.

LEMON CHIFFON

LAYERS: 2
FILLING: Lemon Cream (*see note*)
RATIO*: 1:1
FROSTING: None
OTHER FLOURISHES**:
Dust finished cakes with powdered sugar.

NOTES:
Cut each cake in thirds. Make a lemon cream by folding together 1 recipe Italian Whipped Cream (page 169) and 1 recipe Italian Custard Cream (page 163) and adding the juice and finely grated zest of 2 large lemons. Ice the cakes between the layers with the cream.

RED VELVET CAKE

LAYERS: 2
FILLING: Cream Cheese (page 164)
RATIO*: 1:2
FROSTING: Cream Cheese (page 164)

NOTES:
Fill the cake with cream cheese frosting and ice with the same.

CARROT CAKE

LAYERS: 2
FILLING: Cream Cheese (page 164)
RATIO*: 1:2
FROSTING: Cream Cheese (page 164)

NOTES:
Fill the cake with cream cheese frosting and ice with the same.

CHOCOLATE CHIFFON

{ MAKES TWO 10-INCH CAKES }

For this cake, you will need two 10-inch Bundt or Bundt-style pans, 3 inches deep. Note that they should be aluminum, and must not be nonstick or the cakes will collapse while cooling.

6 extra-large eggs, separated

1½ cups sugar

¾ cup plus 1½ tablespoons cake flour

¾ cup water

½ cup vegetable oil

2½ tablespoons unsweetened Dutch-process cocoa powder

2¼ teaspoons baking powder

1¼ teaspoon fine sea salt

1 teaspoon pure vanilla extract

½ teaspoon baking soda

Distilled white vinegar, for wiping the bowl

1. Position a rack in the center of the oven, and preheat to 350°F.

2. Put the egg yolks, 1 cup of the sugar, the flour, 6 tablespoons of the water, the oil, cocoa, baking powder, salt, vanilla, and baking soda in the bowl of a stand mixer fitted with the whip attachment. (If you don't have a stand mixer, you can use a hand mixer.) Beat starting on low speed, then raise to medium and whip until the mixture is thick and shiny and has multiplied several times in volume, approximately 5 minutes. Pour in the remaining water in a thin stream just until absorbed by the mixture. It will seem watery, but that's okay. Transfer to another bowl and set aside. Wipe out the mixer bowl with vinegar.

3. Put the egg whites in the bowl of the stand mixer and whip for 30 seconds on high speed. With the motor running, add the remaining ½ cup sugar and whip on high until stiff peaks form, 5 to 6 minutes.

4. Fold half the white mixture into the yolk mixture, a little at a time, until uniformly combined. Then pour the combined mixture into the white mixture bowl and fold with a rubber spatula.

5. Do not grease the pans for this recipe. Run some cold water into the pans, rotate them, and shake out the water over the sink. Pour the batter into the pans (it will come about ¾ of the way up the sides), and bake until firm and spongy, 30 to 40 minutes.

6. Remove from the oven and let cool slightly.

7. Manually loosen the cakes by hand from the sides and center tube of the pans, then invert and spank the pan to loosen the cake.

The cakes can be refrigerated in an airtight container for up to 3 days, or may be wrapped in plastic wrap and frozen for up to 2 months.

RED VELVET CAKE

MAKES TWO 9-INCH CAKES OR 24 CUPCAKES

This classic of the American South is just as popular in Hoboken, New Jersey. I never frost this with anything other than Cream Cheese Frosting (page 164).

1¼ cups vegetable shortening
2 cups sugar, plus more for sprinkling the parchment paper
1 tablespoon unsweetened Dutch-process cocoa powder
4½ teaspoons (2 tubes) red food-coloring gel
3 cups cake flour, plus more for flouring the cake pans
1¼ teaspoons fine sea salt
1¼ teaspoons pure vanilla extract
1¼ teaspoons baking soda
1¼ teaspoons distilled white vinegar
3 extra-large eggs
1¼ cups buttermilk
Unsalted butter (about 2 tablespoons), nonstick spray,
or vegetable oil, for greasing the cake pans

1. Position a rack in the center of the oven, and preheat to 350°F.

2. Put the shortening, sugar, cocoa, food coloring, flour, salt, vanilla, bak-
    ing soda, and vinegar in the bowl of a stand mixer fitted with the paddle
    attachment. (You can use a hand mixer if you allow the shortening to soften
    at room temperature before beginning.) Paddle, starting at low speed, then
    raise the speed to low-medium and mix for about 1 minute. Add the eggs,
    one at a time, mixing for 1 minute after each is absorbed into the mixture.
    Add the buttermilk in two portions, stopping to scrape the sides of the
    bowl between additions.

3. Grease two 9-inch cake pans (2 inches deep) with the butter, and flour them
    (see "To Flour a Cake Pan," page 133).

4. Divide the batter evenly between the two cake pans, using a rubber spatula to scrape down the bowl and get as much batter as possible out.

5. Bake until the cakes begin to pull from the sides of the pans and are springy to the touch, 35 to 40 minutes.

6. Remove from the oven and let cool for at least 30 minutes, preferably 1 hour. The cakes should be at room temperature before you remove them from the pan.

7. Put a piece of parchment paper on a cookie sheet, sprinkle with sugar, and one at a time, turn the pans over and turn the cakes out onto the parchment; the sugar will keep them from sticking.

Refrigerate or freeze (see page 92) until ready to decorate.

CARROT CAKE

{ MAKES TWO 9-INCH CAKES OR 24 CUPCAKES }

Golden raisins and walnuts add bursts of sweetness and texture to this classic cake. Note that the carrots carry a lot of moisture, so squeeze out their excess liquid by putting them in a colander and pressing on them with a paper towel after grating to keep the batter from being too wet or loose.

3 cups finely grated carrots (from about 5 large carrots)
2½ cups cake flour, plus more for flouring the cake pans
2 cups sugar, plus more for unmolding the cakes
2 cups Italian Custard Cream (page 163; optional)
¾ cup vegetable oil
2¼ teaspoons baking powder
2 teaspoons ground cinnamon
1 teaspoon baking soda
1 teaspoon pure vanilla extract
½ teaspoon fine sea salt
4 extra-large eggs
1 cup milk
½ cup chopped walnuts
¼ cup golden raisins
Unsalted butter (about 2 tablespoons), nonstick spray,
or vegetable oil, for greasing the cake pans

1. Position a rack in the center of the oven, and preheat to 350°F.

2. Put the carrots, flour, sugar, custard (if using), oil, baking powder, cinnamon, baking soda, vanilla, and salt in the bowl of a stand mixer fitted with the paddle attachment. (If you don't have a stand mixer, you can use a hand mixer.) Mix on low just until the ingredients are tossed together well, a few seconds, then raise the speed to low-medium and continue to mix until the mixture is smooth, approximately 1 additional minute.

3. With the motor running, add one egg at a time, adding the next one after the previous one has been absorbed. Stop the motor periodically and

155

scrape from the bottom of the bowl with a rubber spatula to incorporate. Return the mixer to low-medium speed.

4. Continue to mix for 1 additional minute to ensure that the eggs are fully absorbed. This will also help ensure that all the sugar is dissolved and the flour is incorporated, which will help produce a luxurious mouthfeel in the final cake.

5. With the motor running, pour in the milk, ½ cup at a time, stopping the motor to scrape the sides and bottom of the bowl between the two additions. Continue to mix for another 1 minute or until the mixture appears smooth. Add the walnuts and raisins and mix just to integrate them.

6. Grease two 9-inch cake pans with the butter, and flour them. (For more, see "To Flour a Cake Pan," page 133.)

7. Divide the batter evenly between the two cake pans, using a rubber spatula to scrape down the bowl and get as much batter as possible out. Before baking, be sure the batter is between 70° and 73°F, or the cakes will crown. (Test by plunging a kitchen thermometer into the center of the batter; if it is too warm, put the bowl in the refrigerator for a few minutes; if too cool, let it rest at room temperature.)

8. Bake until the cake begins to pull from the sides of the pan and is springy to the touch, 25 to 30 minutes.

9. Remove from the oven and let cool for at least 30 minutes, preferably 1 hour. The cake should be at room temperature before you remove it from the pan.

10. Put a piece of parchment paper on a cookie sheet, sprinkle with sugar, and one at a time, turn the pans over and turn the cakes out onto the parchment; the sugar will keep them from sticking.

11. Refrigerate or freeze (see page 84) until ready to decorate.

Frostings and Fillings

When you get right down to it, fillings and frostings are where every cake's success begins and ends. So the best way to take a cake from simple to spectacular is to pick the very best combinations. Here, I offer recipes for our most called on fillings and frostings, as well as the combinations that will help you knock it out of the park. But don't let my choices limit you: create your own combinations and— who knows—you might come up with a new classic of your own.

VANILLA FROSTING

{ MAKES ABOUT 4 CUPS, ENOUGH TO FILL & ICE ONE 9-INCH CAKE }

For a creamier frosting, use milk instead of water. You must refrigerate this frosting, as well as any cakes filled or iced with it. Let it come to room temperature before using, and whisk briefly by hand to refresh it.

2½ cups (5 sticks) unsalted butter, softened

5 cups powdered (10X) sugar

1 tablespoon pure vanilla extract

¼ teaspoon fine sea salt

3 tablespoons lukewarm water

1. Put the butter in the bowl of a stand mixer fitted with the paddle attachment and mix on low speed until butter is smooth with no lumps. With the motor running, add the sugar, 1 cup at a time, adding the next cup only after the first addition has been integrated into the mixture.
2. Stop the machine and add the vanilla and salt. Paddle on low-medium speed until completely smooth, approximately 2 minutes. Add the water and continue to mix until light and fluffy, 2 to 3 minutes.

The frosting can be kept in an airtight container at room temperature for up to 2 days.

CHOCOLATE FUDGE FROSTING

{ MAKES ABOUT 4 CUPS, ENOUGH TO FILL & ICE ONE 9-INCH CAKE }

For a creamier frosting, use milk instead of water. You must refrigerate this frosting, as well as any cakes filled or iced with it. Let it come to room temperature before using, and whisk briefly by hand to refresh it.

2½ cups (5 sticks) unsalted butter, softened
5 cups powdered (10X) sugar
⅓ cup unsweetened Dutch-process cocoa powder
1 tablespoon pure vanilla extract
¼ teaspoon fine sea salt
3 tablespoons lukewarm water

1. Put the butter in the bowl of a stand mixer fitted with the paddle attachment and paddle on low speed until smooth, with no lumps, approximately 3 minutes. With the motor running, add the sugar, one cup at a time, adding the next cup only after the first addition is absorbed.
2. Stop the machine and add the cocoa, vanilla, and salt. Paddle on low-medium speed until completely smooth, approximately 2 minutes. Add the water and continue to paddle until light and fluffy, 2 to 3 minutes.

The frosting will keep for up to 2 days in an airtight container at room temperature.

ITALIAN BUTTERCREAM
{ MAKES ABOUT 7 CUPS }

I adapted this recipe from one used at The Culinary Institute of America, shown to me by a group of students for whom I did a demonstration.

8 extra-large egg whites
2 cups sugar
½ cup water
4 cups (8 sticks) unsalted butter, at room temperature, cut into small cubes
1 tablespoon pure vanilla extract

1. Put the whites in the bowl of a stand mixer fitted with the whip attachment.

2. Put 1½ cups of the sugar and the water in a heavy saucepan and bring to a boil over medium-high heat, stirring with a wooden spoon to dissolve the sugar. Continue to cook, without stirring, and bring to the soft ball stage (240°F).

3. Meanwhile, whip the whites at high speed until soft peaks form, approximately 5 minutes. With the motor running, add the remaining ½ cup sugar gradually, continuing to whip until medium peaks form.

4. When the sugar reaches 240°F, with the motor running, pour it into the egg whites, very slowly, in a thin stream, to avoid cooking the eggs. Raise the speed to high, and continue to whip until the mixture has cooled to room temperature, 10 to 15 minutes.

5. Stopping the motor between additions, add the butter in 5 increments, scraping the bowl with a rubber spatula before adding each addition of butter. With the motor running, add the vanilla, and whip just until it is blended in.

The buttercream can be refrigerated in an airtight container for up to 1 week. Let it come to room temperature and paddle briefly before using.

ITALIAN CUSTARD CREAM
{ MAKES ABOUT 3 CUPS, ENOUGH TO FILL
AND ICE ONE 9-INCH CAKE }

The longer you cook this cream, the thicker it will become, so you can—and should—adjust the texture to suit your taste.

2½ cups whole milk
1 tablespoon pure vanilla extract
1 cup sugar
⅓ cup cake flour, sifted
5 extra-large egg yolks
2 teaspoons salted butter

1. Put the milk and vanilla in a saucepan and bring to a simmer over medium heat.

2. In a bowl, whip together the sugar, flour, and egg yolks with a hand mixer. Ladle a cup of the milk-vanilla mixture into the bowl and beat to temper the yolks.

3. Add the yolk mixture to the pot and beat over medium heat with the hand mixer until thick and creamy, about 1 minute. As you are beating, move the pot on and off the flame so that you don't scramble the eggs.

4. Remove the pot from the heat, add the butter, and whip for 2 minutes to thicken the cream. Transfer to a bowl. Let cool, cover with plastic wrap, and refrigerate at least 6 hours.

Will keep for up to 1 week.

To make chocolate custard cream, add 1½ ounces melted, cooled unsweetened chocolate along with the butter. For a richer chocolate flavor, add a little more.

CREAM CHEESE FROSTING

{ MAKES ABOUT 3 CUPS, ENOUGH TO
FILL AND ICE ONE 9-INCH CAKE }

*I always make this frosting—the classic filling and topping
for Carrot Cake (page 155) and Red Velvet Cake (page 153)—with
Philadelphia brand cream cheese, which I think is simply the best.*

Use this as soon as you make it because it gets very stiff in the refrigerator. If you have to refrigerate it, do not microwave it to freshen it. Instead, let it rest at room temperature for 4 hours to soften.

Two 8-ounce packages cream cheese
½ cup (1 stick) unsalted butter, softened
1 teaspoon pure vanilla extract
2 cups powdered (10X) sugar, sifted

1. Put the cream cheese and butter in the bowl of a stand mixer fitted with the paddle attachment and paddle at medium speed until creamy, approximately 30 seconds.

2. With the motor running, pour in the vanilla and paddle for 30 seconds. Add the sugar, a little at a time, and mix until smooth, approximately 1 minute after the last addition.

Use right away, or refrigerate in an airtight container for up to 2 days.

MY DAD'S CHOCOLATE MOUSSE

{ MAKES ABOUT 3½ CUPS, ENOUGH TO FILL AND ICE ONE 9-INCH CAKE }

This chocolate whipped cream, which we still make with my Dad's recipe, is fluffy and rich, and gets along with a wide range of cakes and fillings.

2 cups heavy cream
½ cup sugar
3 tablespoons unsweetened Dutch-process cocoa powder
1 tablespoon Kahlúa or coffee liqueur

Put the cream, sugar, cocoa powder, and Kahlúa in a stainless-steel mixing bowl.
Blend with a hand mixer at high speed until fluffy, about 1 minute.
Use immediately or refrigerate in an airtight container for up to 3 days.

CHOCOLATE GANACHE

{ MAKES ABOUT 2 CUPS }

This ganache can be used as a filling and/or poured over a cake. To use it as a filling, refrigerate it, transfer it to a pastry bag, and pipe it out following the directions on page 88.

To pour ganache over a cake, melt it in a double boiler and simply pour it over a cake or layer. To top layers of French cream or chocolate mousse with ganache, pour it on and smooth it with a cake icing spatula.

1 cup heavy cream
9 ounces semisweet chocolate, coarsely chopped
1 tablespoon light corn syrup

1. Put the heavy cream in a saucepan and set it over medium-high heat. As soon as it begins to simmer, remove the pot from the heat. Add the chocolate and stir with a wooden spoon to melt the chocolate. Stir in the corn syrup.

2. To cover a cake with poured ganache, set a wire rack in or over a baking tray. Set the cake on the rack. Carefully ladle the molten ganache over the cake in a steady stream, letting it run over the cake until uniformly covered.

3. Otherwise, transfer to a bowl and refrigerate for about 1 hour. If using for filling, soften in a double boiler over medium heat until pourable.

4. Let any unused ganache cool, transfer to an airtight container, and refrigerate for up to 3 days. Reheat gently in a double boiler set over simmering water, stirring with a rubber spatula until warm and pourable.

LOBSTER TAIL
CREAM

{ MAKES 5½ CUPS }

We use this decadent cream to fill our signature lobster tail pastries, but it can also be used to fill and/or frost cakes; it's especially delicious on our Vanilla Cake (page 134).

The amount of Bailey's Irish Cream is negligible, but it adds a subtle elegance.

Italian Custard Cream (page 163)
Italian Whipped Cream (page 169)
2 tablespoons Bailey's Irish Cream liqueur,
  plus more to taste (optional)

1. Put the custard cream in a mixing bowl. Add the whipped cream, a little at a time, folding it in with a rubber spatula.

2. Drizzle the Bailey's Irish Cream (if using), over the mixture, gently mixing it in. Add more to taste, if desired, but do not overmix the cream.

The cream can be refrigerated in an airtight container for up to 4 days. Whisk briefly by hand to refresh before using.

ITALIAN WHIPPED CREAM

{ MAKES ABOUT 2½ CUPS }

This sweetened whipped cream can be used to fill and/or ice cakes, and is also a component of French cream and lobster cream.

1½ cups heavy cream
¼ cup plus 2 tablespoons sugar

Put the cream and sugar in a bowl and whip on high speed with a hand mixer. Do not overmix or you'll end up with butter.

The cream can be refrigerated in an airtight container for up to 3 days. Whisk by hand to refresh before using.

SYRUP

{ MAKES 5½ CUPS }

Use this recipe to make syrups to soak the Pan di Spagna on page 142. In addition to the liqueurs called for in the book, you can use the formula to create other syrups. A good rule of thumb for selecting a brand of liqueur is to pick what you like to drink, and steer away from the cheap stuff.

For a stronger flavor, increase the amount of liqueur up to ½ cup.

1 cup water
1 cup sugar
¼ cup liqueur, such as Rosolio, Strega, or rum (see Note below)

Put the water, sugar, and liqueur into a saucepan and bring to a simmer over medium-high heat. Whisk until the sugar dissolves, approximately 3 to 4 minutes. Let cool before using.

The syrup may be refrigerated in an airtight container for up to 2 weeks.

NOTE:
Rosolio and Strega can be hard to find. There is no truly comparable replacement for them, but you can substitute other sweet liqueurs if you cannot get your hands on them.

Acknowledgments

Nobody writes a book by himself, and I'd like to thank the following people for their help on this project, and in the growing family of *Cake Boss* shows:

My wife, Lisa. Thank you for sharing all the great adventures with me, both the wonderful and wild ride we've enjoyed with *Cake Boss*, and the even greater adventure of Life. There's nobody I'd rather have as my partner through it all. I love you.

My Sofia Bear, Buddy, Marco, and Carlo—my four incredible kids. You guys make me proud every day, and continue to be my inspiration—you're why I get out of bed and go to work every morning, and the reason I can't wait to come home at the end of the day.

My father, Buddy Valastro, the original Cake Boss. As it says on that picture in our bakery, you may be gone, but you are not forgotten. We all miss you, and work to honor you every day of our lives.

Mary Valastro (Mama). You may not be as involved with Carlo's Bake Shop as you used to be, but your presence is still felt there every minute of every day, and the personal and professional examples you set will guide me always.

My four big sisters, Grace, Madeline, Mary, and Lisa. It's tough to put words to how much I care about the four of you. You've been there, literally, my entire life and I love knowing you're there, in my corner, every day of the year.

My brothers-in-law, Mauro, Joey, and Joe. You guys will always be like the brothers I never had. As far as I'm concerned, we should just drop the "in-law"—you're my real brothers. I have to also give tremendous, special thanks to Joey for testing the recipes for this book—and in his own home kitchen, no less. (I don't know how he talked my sister Grace into letting him do that, but I was impressed that he did!)

The crew at the bakery for helping the place run like a well-oiled machine, especially Frankie and Danny, and special thanks to Frankie, Liz, Rachael, and Melanie for their help with the photo shoots for this book. Also, a huge appreciative shout-out to German for helping with the recipe testing.

Adam Bourcier, thanks for all the help on the book, and for continuing to help manage this empire's growth. We've got big things on the horizon and I'm happy to have you on the team.

Nikky O'Connell, my personal assistant. You do so much, and I appreciate all of it. I couldn't accomplish what I do without you.

Sal Picinich. A lot of the wisdom in this book I learned from you. I miss you, but I'm comforted to know that you're in heaven, baking with my dad.

Andrew Friedman. Once again, you've taken my thoughts and magically transferred them to the page. I'm happy to call you my friend.

Marcus Nilsson, thanks for your great photography and for being a pleasure to work with on those long shoot days. To Stephanie Hanes for her lovely prop styling. And to Bridget Stoyko, Melissa Stonehill, and Tracy Collins for their expert production and management of the photo shoots.

The team at my publisher: our editor, Leslie Meredith, for her continued support and encouragement; publisher Judith Curr for her abiding belief; associate editor Donna Loffredo for her help during the editing and production stage.

Jon Rosen and the team at William Morris Endeavor Entertainment. Thanks for a truly fantastic year; can't wait to see what we pull off next!

Erin Niumata of Folio Literary Management, who agented this book—thanks for your friendship and for making this project happen the right way. And my lasting appreciation to Maura Teitelbaum at Abrams Artists Agency for her early direction and guidance.

The Brooks Group, Carlo's Bake Shop's public relations agency—thanks for getting the word out about all the exciting news we've had over the last year, and for your terrific advice and enthusiasm along the way.

To my extended family—my aunts and uncles, cousins and second cousins—and to all my friends (you know who you are), thanks for everything and for helping me stay grounded during these life-changing couple of years.

The loyal customers of Carlo's Bake Shop—thanks for lining up to visit us, and for all the enthusiasm you bring to our shop. When we bake and decorate, we think of you and how much pleasure we hope our products bring to you.

I have to also thank God, for giving me a blessed life—my family and our business would have been riches enough for any man; all the rest is just the icing on the cake.

And to the rest of my extended family at TLC and Discovery: David Zaslav, president and CEO, Discovery Communications; Eileen O'Neill, group president, Discovery and TLC Networks; Joe Abruzzese, president, Advertising Sales, US Networks; Nancy Daniels, EVP, Production and Development, Discovery Channel; Howard Lee, SVP, Production and Development, TLC; Dustin Smith, VP, Communications, TLC; Sue Perez-Jackson, director, Licensing, Discovery Communications; Edward Sabin, group COO, Discovery and TLC Networks; and Jen Williams, VP, Talent Management and Strategy. And two essential figures who no longer work on the show, but who helped shape it and its success: John Paul Stoops and Jon Sechrist. I love working with all of you. Thank you for helping me realize my dreams and for all we have achieved together, and will continue to achieve in the future.

To my fans. Without you guys, I wouldn't be the Cake Boss. Thanks for watching, for writing, for coming to the live shows, and for buying my books. You're the best and I love you all.

Index

About the Author

Buddy Valastro is the author of the *New York Times* bestsellers *Cake Boss* and *Baking with the Cake Boss,* as well as *Cooking Italian with the Cake Boss,* and star of the hit TLC series *Cake Boss, Next Great Baker,* and *Bakery Boss.* He is owner and operator of Carlo's Bakery in Hoboken, New Jersey, with multiple Carlo's Bake Shops in the surrounding area. In addition, Buddy operates the Cake Boss Cafe in Times Square, New York City. He lives in New Jersey with his wife and four children.